DAILY OFFICE ENGLISH CONVERSATION

Preface

중학교 3년, 고등학교 3년, 대학을 거쳐 10년 넘게 영어공부를 하고 있다.

하지만 본인의 영어실력을 묻는 질문에 자신 있게 "上"이라고 이야기하지 못하는 경우가 많은 것 또한 사실이다. 왜 그럴까? 우리에게 영어는 시험으로 존재해 왔기 때문이다. 최근 스피킹이 중요시되고는 있지만 여전히 취업의 주요 자격증은 토익이라고 말하고 있다.

이 책은 미국 대학에서 테솔(TESOL)을 전공하고 20년 넘게 대학생들을 가르쳐온 저자와 무역회사에서 체득한 콘텐츠를 바탕으로 실전영어를 가르쳐온 저자가 예비직장인 학생들이 사무영어회화 기본기를 갖출 수 있도록 작성한 결과물이다.

사무실에서 혹은 비즈니스 상황에서 벌어지는 주제별로 핵심문장들을 뽑아냈다. 이 표현들만 내 것으로 만들어도 웬만한 상황에서는 충분히 소통이 가능할 것이다. 언어도 진화한다는 사실을 염두에 두어 현지 외국인의 자문을 받아 최신 영어 표현을 담았다.

1장은 기본적인 인사와 소개를 담고 있으며, 2장은 사무실에서 벌어지는 일상업무와 관련한 내용을 다루고 있다. 3장은 비즈니스 영어회화의 기본인 전화 업무를 다루었고, 4장은 대면 회의의 개최, 변경, 취소 등의 내용을 담고 있다. 또한 최근 빈번해진 온라인 미팅에 대한 꿀팁을 제공한다. 5장은 비즈니스 출장에 필요한 항공편, 호텔 예약, 렌터카, 한국문화 소개 등을 다루고 있으며, 마지막으로 6장은 비즈니스 이메일 작성에 필요한 포맷과 구성요소를 샘플 이메일과 함께 제시하고 있다.

이 책을 충분히 활용하기 위해서는 각 Unit의 Words and Phrases를 통해 단어와 숙어를 먼저 익힌 후 Warm-up Dialogue를 통해 핵심 대화를 이해하고, Key Expressions을 통해 꼭 알아야 할 표현들을 학습한 후에 상황별 Conversation과 Pattern Drill로 마무리하여 학

습의 완성도를 높이는 것이 효과적이다. 각 장마다 회화 시 필요한 기본 문법과 어휘 활용, 연습문제와 롤 플레이 등 다양한 활동을 할 수 있도록 구성함으로써 대학교재로서의 효과성을 높였다.

아무쪼록 이 책을 통해 기본 사무영어에 대한 "두려움"을 "자신감"으로 변화시키기를 바란다.

마지막으로 흔쾌히 자문을 맡아준 Christine 님께 감사의 마음을 전한다. 또한 이 책의 출판을 기꺼이 맡아주신 한올 출판사 임순재 대표님과 관계자 여러분들께 감사를 드린다.

2022년 1월

저자 김숙경
양혜련

Contents

Daily Office English Conversation
사무영어회화

Chapter 01

Greetings & Introductions

Unit 1 Greetings

Words and Phrases

- greet 인사하다
- fine / great 좋아요
- so so / not so bad 그저 그래요
- nothing special / same as always 별일 없어요
- never been better / couldn't be better 아주 좋아요
- long time no see 오랜만이에요
- look forward to+동사원형+ing ~을 고대(기대)하다
- get in touch / keep in touch 연락하다
- give my best regards to~ / say hello to ~에게 안부 전해주세요

Warm up Dialogue

인사하기	응답하기
• Good morning.	• Good morning.
• How are you doing?	• Pretty good, thanks. And you?
• How do you do?	• How do you do?
• How have you been lately?	• I've been busy lately.
• Nice to meet you.	• Glad to meet you, too.

Key Expressions

- 좋은 아침 / 오후 / 저녁 / 밤입니다.
  Good morning.
  Good afternoon.
  Good evening.
  Good night.

- 안녕하세요 / 안녕
  Hello!
  Hi!

- 잘 지내시나요?
  How are you?
  How are you doing?
  How is it going?

- 어떻게 지내셨는지요? (오랜만에 만나는 사람에게 하는 인사)
  How have you been?
  How has everything been with you?

- 처음 뵙겠습니다. (처음 만난 사이에 하는 정중한 인사)
  How do you do?

- 만나서 반갑습니다.
  Nice to meet you.
  Glad / happy / Pleased to meet you.

- 만나 뵙기를 고대합니다.
  I'm looking forward to meeting you.

- 좋습니다.
  Fine / Great / Wonderful / Terrific / Marvelous, thanks.

- 괜찮습니다.
  Not bad, thanks.

- 오랜만이에요.
  Long time no see.
  It's been a long time since we last met.

- 최근에 바빴습니다.
  I've been busy lately.

- 다시 만나서 반가워요.
  It's good to see you again.

- 상사에게 안부 전해주세요.
  Give my best regards to your boss.
  Please say hello to your boss.

- 연락하기로 해요.
  Let's get in touch.
  Keep in touch.

Conversation Greetings

A Hello, James. How are you?
B Great, thanks. And you?

A Very well, thank you. May I introduce my coworker to you?
B Certainly.

A James, let me introduce Paul Kim.
B How do you do, Mr. Kim? Nice to meet you. I'm James Stewart.
C How do you do, Mr. Stewart? Pleased to meet you, too.

주요표현 연습(Pattern Drill)

1. 처음 뵙겠습니다.

   _______ do you __________?

2. 만나서 반갑습니다.

   ________ to ________ you.

3. 오래간만입니다.

   _______ time no ________.

4. 만나 뵙기를 고대합니다.

   I'm _________ __________ to __________ you.

5. 상사에게 안부 전해주세요.

   Please _______ _______ to your boss.

Unit 2

Introductions

Words and Phrases

- introduce 소개하다
- mobile phone / cellular phone 휴대폰
- email address 이메일 주소
- office worker 사무원
- accountant 회계사
- lawyer 변호사
- sales manager 영업 부장
- engineer 기술자, 엔지니어
- department 부서
- investment company 투자회사
- in charge of ~을 담당하다
- personal information 개인 정보
- work-related 업무와관련된

Warm up Dialogue Introductions 1

개인정보 질문하기	응답하기
• What's your (full) name? • What is your last name? • What is your first name? • What is your cell / mobile phone number? • What is your email address?	• My name is Gina Kim / Kim Gina. • My last name is Kim. • My first name is Gina. • My cell phone number is 010-123-4567. • My email address is ginakim@snh.com.

Key Expressions

- 안녕하세요. 저는 Larry Smith입니다.
  Hello. My name is Larry Smith.
- 제 소개를 하겠습니다.
  Let me introduce myself.
  I'd like to introduce myself.
- 당신의 이름은 무엇입니까?
  What is your name?
- 성은 무엇입니까?
  What is your last name?
- 이름은 무엇입니까?
  What is your first name?
- 당신의 사무실 전화번호 / 휴대폰 번호는 무엇입니까?
  What is your office phone number?
  What is your cell / mobile phone number?
- 당신의 이메일 주소는 무엇입니까?
  What is your email address?
- 제 이름은 김지나입니다.
  My name is Gina Kim / Kim Gina.
- 제 성은 김입니다.
  My last name is Kim.
- 제 이름은 지나입니다.
  My first name is Gina.
- 사무실번호는 02-555-3377입니다.
  My office number is 02-555-3377.
  It's 02-555-3377.
- 제 휴대폰 번호는 010-123-4567입니다.
  My cell phone number is 010-123-4567.
  It's 010-123-4567.
- 제 이메일 주소는 ginakim@snh.com입니다.
  My email address is ginakim@snh.com.

Warm up Dialogue Introductions 2

업무 관련 질문하기	응답하기
• What do you do?	• I am an office worker.
• What company do you work for?	• I work for SNH Company. • I work at SNH Company.
• Which department are you in?	• I work in the Accounting Department.
• What line are you in?	• I am in the Marketing Department.

Key Expressions

- 무슨 일을 하세요?
  What do you do?
- 어떤 회사에서 일하세요?
  What company do you work for?
  What is the name of your company?
- 무슨 부서에서 일하세요?
  Which department are you in?
  What line are you in?
- 사무직원입니다.
  I am an office worker.
- 리셉셔니스트(접수 담당자)입니다.
  I am a receptionist.
- 회계사입니다.
  I'm an accountant.
- 오피스매니저입니다.
  I am an office manager.
- 컴퓨터 프로그래머입니다.
  I am a computer programmer.
- 엔지니어입니다.
  I am an engineer.
- 저는 투자회사에 다닙니다.
  I work for an investment company.
- 저는 SNH사에 다닙니다.
  I work at SNH Company.
- 회계부서 / 영업부서에서 일합니다.
  I work in the Accounting Department.
  I work in the Sales Department.
- 저는 사무직을 맡고 있습니다.
  I am in charge of clerical work.

Conversation Introductions

A Hello, Gina. Long time no see. How have you been?
B Hi, Paul. It's been a long time since we last met.

A You work at SNH Company, right?
B Yes. What company do you work for?

A I work for ABC Company. I'm a sales manager. Which department do you work in?
B I work in the General Affairs Department. I am in charge of clerical work.

A What is your email address?
B My email address is ginakim@snh.com.

주요표현 연습(Pattern Drill)

1. 성이 무엇입니까? / 박 씨입니다.

   ________ is your ________ name?

   My ________ ________ is Park.

2. 무슨 일을 하십니까? / 저는 오피스 매니저입니다.

   ________ do you ________?

   I ________ ________ office manager.

3. 어떤 회사에서 일하십니까? / 저는 SNH Company에서 일합니다.

   What ____________ do you ________ for?

   I ________ ________ SNH Company.

4. 무슨 부서에서 일하십니까? / 영업부서에서 일합니다.

   What __________ are you _______?

   I _______ in _______ _________ Department.

5. 당신의 이메일 주소는 무엇입니까? / 제 이메일 주소는 ginakim@snh.com입니다.

   _______ is _______ email address?

   _______ e-mail ________ is ginakim@snh.com.

Unit 3

Small Talk

Words and Phrases

- How's the weather today? 오늘 날씨가 어떤가요?
- It's rainy / cloudy / snowy / sunny / stormy. 비 오는 / 흐린 / 눈 오는 / 화창한 / 폭풍우가 치는
- It's beautiful today. 날씨가 좋습니다
- free time / spare time 여가시간
- activity 활동
- favorite 좋아하는
- play sports 운동경기 하다
- watch soccer / baseball games 축구 / 야구 경기를 보다
- take a picture 사진 찍다
- enjoy+동사원형+ing ~을 즐기다
- playing the piano 피아노 연주
- surfing the Internet 인터넷 서핑(탐색)
- reading books 독서

Warm up Dialogue

여가 활동 묻기	응답하기
• What do you do when you are free? • What is your free time activity?	• I enjoy surfing the Internet. • My free / spare time activity is reading books.
• What's the weather like today?	• It's beautiful. • It's sunny and cool.

Key Expressions

- 여가시간에 무엇을 하세요?
  What do you do when you are free?
- 취미가 무엇인가요?
  What is your hobby?
  What is your free time activity?
- 저는 여가시간에 인터넷 서핑을 즐겨요.
  I enjoy surfing the Internet when I am free.
- 저는 여가시간에 책 읽는 것을 좋아합니다.
  I love reading books when I am free.
  My free time activity is reading books.
- 제 취미는 피아노 연주입니다.
  My hobby is playing the piano.
- 축구경기 보는 것을 좋아합니다.
  I enjoy watching soccer games.

Conversation Small talk

A It's beautiful today, isn't it?
B That's right. It's sunny and cool.

A What do you do in your spare time?
B I enjoy surfing the Internet when I am free. How about you?

A I like to take pictures of the nature. I spend most of my free time taking pictures in the mountains and valleys where nature is beautiful.
B Sounds interesting!

주요표현 연습(Pattern Drill)

1. 여가시간에 무엇을 하세요?
   ________ do you ________ when you are ________?

2. 저는 야구경기를 보는 것을 좋아합니다.
   I ________ ___________ baseball games.

3. 당신의 취미는 무엇인가요?
   ________ is your ________?

4. 제 취미는 기타 연주입니다.

My ________ is ________ the guitar.

5. 저는 자연을 찍으며 대부분의 여가시간을 보냅니다.

I ________ most of my free time ________ pictures of the nature.

Grammar Point

❶ 'Be' 동사의 현재(Simple present)

Simple present tense verb 'be'

statement	contractions	questions	negatives	contractions
I am	I'm	Am I … ?	I am not …	I'm not …
You are	You're	Are you … ?	You are not …	You're not …
She / He / It is	She's / He's / It's	Is he / she / it ?	He / She / It is not …	He / She / It isn't …
We are	We're	Are we … ?	We are not …	We're not …
They are	They're	Are they … ?	They are not …	They're not …

Wh-Questions and Answers(의문사 의문문)

Wh-word	Be verb	Subject	Answers
Who	are	you?	I am Gina Kim.
What	is	your first name?	Gina.
Where	are	you from?	I am from Seoul, Korea.
When	is	your birthday?	It is on December 25th.
Why	are	you late?	I missed my bus.
How	is	your work?	It is interesting.

❷ 주격대명사

주어를 대신하여 사용하는 대명사로 인칭대명사와 비 인칭대명사로 구분한다.

- 인칭대명사: 사람을 지칭하는 대명사(I, You, He, She, They, We)
- 비 인칭대명사: 사람을 제외한 사물, 동물 등에 쓰이는 대명사(It, They)

대명사 종류	주격	소유격
1인칭(단수)	I	my
2인칭(단수)	you	your
3인칭(단수, 남성)	he	his
3인칭(단수, 여성)	she	her
3인칭(단수, 사물, 동물)	it	its

대명사 종류	주격	소유격
1인칭(복수)	we	our
2인칭(복수)	you	your
3인칭(복수)	they	their

❸ 의문사의 종류

- Who – ask about people(사람)
- When – ask about times & dates(시간, 날짜)
- Where – ask about places(장소)
- What – ask about things(사물)
- Why – ask about the reason for something(이유)
- How – ask about the way of something(방법)

Practicing on Your Own

Ⓐ Complete the sentences with *is*, *am*, or *are*. (알맞은 be동사를 넣어 문장을 완성하세요)

1. He ________ at work.
2. They ________ at home.
3. I ________ in class.
4. She ________ at school.
5. They ________ from Japan.
6. It ________ on the desk.
7. You ________ from India.
8. I ________ twenty.
9. You ________ so friendly.
10. It ________ Saturday.

B **Rewrite these sentences with *he*, *she*, *it* or *they*.** (주어를 대명사로 고쳐 쓰세요)

Ex. My brother and I are high school students. → We are high school students.

1. Mary is a college student. → ______________________.

2. Tom is an office worker. → ______________________.

3. Peter and I are friends. → ______________________.

4. Sue and Helen are sisters. → ______________________.

5. Today is Friday. → ______________________.

Language Check

A **Match each question with the correct answer.** (질문에 알맞은 대답을 연결하세요)

1. Where are you from?	a. Yes, I have.
2. What do you do?	b. Yes, I do.
3. Who do you work for?	c. I'm from Japan.
4. Where do you live?	d. I'm an engineer.
5. Have you ever been to Korea?	e. IBM.
6. Do you like Seoul?	f. Seoul, Korea.

B **Write the questions in the Simple Present Tense.** (괄호 안의 주어를 이용하여 의문사 의문문으로 만드세요)

Ex. Who / work for? (you) --> Who do you work for?

1. What / do? (your brother)

____

2. Where / work? (you)

____

3. How old / be? (they)

____

4. What / do in your spare time? (you)

____

5. Where / be from? (your parents)

____

Work in Pairs

A **Interview three other students and write notes in the spaces provided. Use the Personal Information Survey below for activity.** (다른 세 명의 학생과 인터뷰 한 후 주어진 칸을 채우세요. 활동을 위해 개인정보 조사지를 이용하세요)

Personal Information Survey

	Partner 1	Partner 2	Partner 3
1. Name What's your...?			
2. Home town Where are ?			
3. People in family How many...?			
4. Job What do...?			
5. Interests / hobbies What are...? What do you...?			
6. Phone number What is...?			

Sample Questions & Answers

Question 1 What's your name?

Answer 1 My name is __________.

Question 2 Where are you from? Where is your hometown?

Answer 2 I'm from __________.

Question 3 How many people are there in your family?

Answer 3 There are four members in my family. They are father, mother, brother and myself.

Question 4 What do you do?

Answer 4 I am a student.

Question 5 What do you do in your free time? What is your free time activity?

Answer 5 I enjoy surfing the internet.

Question 6 What is your cell phone number?

Answer 6 My cell phone number is 010-234-5678.

B **Look at the business card and introduce yourself.** (명함을 보고 당신을 소개하는 연습입니다. 마지막 빈 카드에 당신의 명함을 만들고 소개하세요)

Gina Kim Office Manager ***SNH Company*** mobile 010-5555-7319 ginakim@snh.com	**James Stewart** Computer Programmer ***Cheil Electronics*** 5F Dong-A Bldg. Insadong, Chongnogu Seoul, Korea mobile 010-5655-9640 james_stewart@cheil_elelectro.com
Paul Kim Sales & Marketing Director ***ABC Company*** 123 Samsungdong, Gangnamgu Seoul, Korea mobile 010-6267-1369 paulkim@abc.com	

타 문화 이해하기(Understanding Other Culture)

악수매너

Shaking Hands: Eye contact is very important(a sign of honesty).

- Shake hands firmly(but not strongly).
- Shake hands last a few seconds.

가벼운 대화 매너

Small Talk: It helps to break the ice when you meet someone for the first time. At its best, it results in a nice first impression being made.

- 적당한 대화주제(Acceptable topics of conversation): weather, sports, hobbies, travel, movies
- 피해야 할 대화주제(Avoid topics of conversation): religion, politics, money, age, personal health, weight

Daily Office English Conversation
사무영어회화

Chapter

02

Daily Routines at the Office

Unit 1 Welcoming Visitors

Words and Phrases

- appointment 약속
- visit 방문, 방문하다
- in regard to ~에 관하여
- expect someone ~를 기다리다
- wait for a moment 잠시 기다리다
- let(you / him / her) know ~에게 알려주다
- meeting / conference 회의
- client 고객
- keep you waiting 당신을 기다리게 하다
- appreciate ~에 대해 감사하다
- have a seat / take a seat 앉다
- Would you like ~하시겠습니까?
- something to drink ~마실 것
- prefer ~을 더 좋아하다(선호하다)
- try 시도하다. 해보다.
- decaffeinated coffee / caffeine-free coffee 카페인이 없는 커피
- Ice coffee 냉커피
- mild 연한, 부드러운
- strong 진한
- slice / piece 조각

Warm up Dialogue

방문 목적 묻기	응답하기
• Good morning. May I help you?	• I came to see Ms. Gina Kim.
• Do you have an appointment?	• I have an appointment at 2:00 p.m.
• Would you please wait for a moment?	• Certainly.
• May I ask what your visit is in regard to?	• I'd like to meet him because I want to explain about our company's new products.

Key Expressions

- 무엇을 도와드릴까요?
  Good morning. May I help you?
  What can I do for you?
- Ms. Gina Kim를 만나러 왔습니다.
  I'm here to see Ms. Gina Kim.
  I came to see Ms. Gina Kim.
- 약속하셨습니까?
  Do you have an appointment?
- 오전 10시에 약속이 되어 있습니다.
  I have an appointment at 10:00 in the morning.
- 성함을 알 수 있을까요?
  May I have your name, please?
- 오신 용건을 말씀해 주시겠습니까?
  May I ask what your visit is in regard to?
- 잠시만 기다려 주시겠습니까?
  Would you please wait for a moment?
- 그에게 / 그녀에게 당신이 오셨다고 말씀드리겠습니다.
  I'll let him / her know you are here.
- Ms. Gina Kim이 기다리고 계십니다.
  Ms. Gina Kim is waiting for you.
  Ms. Gina Kim is expecting you.
- 죄송하지만 Ms. Kim은 회의 중입니다.
  I'm sorry, but Ms. Kim is in a meeting now.
- 죄송하지만 Ms. Kim은 다른 고객을 만나고 있습니다.
  I'm sorry Ms. Kim is with another client now.
- 기다리시게 해서 죄송합니다.
  I'm sorry to keep you waiting.
- 제가 안내해 드리겠습니다.
  I'll show you the way.
- 이쪽으로 오시겠습니까?
  Would you come this way, please?
  This way, please.

Conversation Welcoming visitors

A Good afternoon. May I help you?
B Hello, I'd like to see Ms. Helen Oh. I have an appointment at 2 p.m.

A May I ask your name, please?
B My name is Paul Kim. I arrived a little early.

A Mr. Kim, I'm sorry, but Ms. Oh is in a meeting now. She will be with you in just a minute. Could you wait for a while?
B No problem.

Conversation Receiving visitors

A Good morning. May I help you?
B Hello, I'd like to see Ms. Helen Oh. I have an appointment at 11 a.m.

A May I ask your name, please?
B My name is Paul Kim.

A Mr. Kim, I'll let her know you are here. Just a moment, please.
(Helen? Mr. Paul Kim is here for 11 o'clock appointment.)

A Mr. Kim, Ms. Oh is expecting you. Would you come this way, please?
B Thank you.

주요표현 연습(Pattern Drill)

1. Mr. Kim을 만나러 왔습니다.

I'm __________ to __________ Mr. Kim.

약속하셨습니까?

Do you __________ an ____________________?

2. 네. 저는 2시에 약속하였습니다.

Yes. I __________ an appointment __________ 2 p.m.

성함을 알려 주시겠습니까?

__________ I have your __________, please?

3. 죄송하지만 Mr. Kim은 회의 중입니다.

I'm __________, but Mr. Kim is __________ a __________ now.

오신 용건을 말씀해 주시겠습니까?

May I __________ what your __________ is in __________ to?

4. 잠시만 기다려 주시겠습니까?

Would you please __________ for a __________?

기나리시게 해서 죄송합니다.

I'm sorry to __________ you __________.

5. 그가 당신을 기다리고 있습니다.

He is __________ you.

이쪽으로 오세요.

Would you __________ this __________, please?

Warm up Dialogue

음료 제공하기	응답하기
• Would you like something to drink?	• I would like a cup of coffee.
• Would you prefer coffee or tea?	• Green tea, please.
• May I have some water, please?	• Sure. I'll get you some water.
• How would you like your coffee?	• I like strong one.

Key Expressions

- 여기 앉으세요.
  Please have a seat.
- 기다리시는 동안 마실 것 좀 드릴까요?
  Would you like something to drink while you wait?
- 어떤 음료를 드시겠습니까?
  What would you like to drink?
- 커피 한 잔 드릴까요?
  Would you like some coffee?
- 커피 또는 차 중에서 어느 것을 드시겠습니까?
  Would you prefer coffee or tea?
- 제가 커피를 가져다 드리겠습니다.
  I'll get you some coffee.
- 커피 한잔 더 하시겠어요?
  Would you like some more coffee?
- 다른 필요한 것이 있을까요?
  Do you need anything else?
- 물 좀 주시겠습니까?
  May I have some water, please?
- 당신의 도움에 감사드립니다.
  Thank you very much for your help.
  I really appreciate your help.
- 도와드리게 되어 기쁩니다.
  It's my pleasure.
  Glad to be of help.
- 천만에요.
  No worries.
  You're welcome. Don't mention it.
- 제가 또 도울 일 있으시면 알려주십시오.
  Let me know if I can help out again.
- 만나서 즐거웠습니다.
  I enjoyed meeting with you.
- 곧 다시 뵙게 되기를 바랍니다.
  Hope we'll see you again very soon.
  I look forward to seeing you soon.

Conversation Offering drinks

A Good morning. May I help you?
B I have an appointment with Ms. Gina Kim.
A I'm sorry she is in a meeting now. She will be with you in 5 minutes. Can you have a seat and wait for her?
B No problem.
A Would you like something to drink while you wait?
B Sure, do you have coffee by any chance?
A Yes, I do. I'll get you some coffee.
B Thanks a lot.

주요표현 연습(Pattern Drill)

1. 기다리시는 동안 마실 것 좀 드릴까요?

   Would you like ____________ to drink ____________ you wait?

2. 커피 한 잔 부탁드려도 될까요?

   Do you ____________ coffee by any ____________?

3. 자리에 앉으십시오.

   Please ____________ a ____________.

4. 제가 커피를 가져다 드리겠습니다.

   I'll ____________ you some coffee.

5. 물 좀 주시겠습니까?

   May I ____________ some ____________, please?

Unit 2

Locations & Directions

Words and Phrases

〈Locations〉

- where's the ~? ~은 어디 있나요?
- restaurant 식당
- gym 체육관
- lounge 라운지
- business center 비즈니스센터
- Korean / Japanese / Chinese / Italian restaurant 한식당 / 일식당 / 중식당 / 이탈리안 식당
- on the third floor 3층에
- behind the building 빌딩 뒤에
- next to the building 빌딩 옆에
- in the basement 지하에
- to the right / left of the elevator 엘리베이터 오른쪽(왼쪽)에
- across from the coffee shop 커피숍 건너편에

〈Directions〉

- nearby 근처에, 가까운 곳에
- on the opposite side of ~의 맞은 편에
- turn left / right 왼쪽(오른쪽)으로 돌아가세요.
- go straight 직진하세요.
- go to the corner 모퉁이까지 가세요.
- go two blocks 두 블록(사거리) 가세요.
- on the corner 모퉁이에
- cross the street 길을 건너세요.

Warm up Dialogue

길 묻기	응답하기
• Where's the Korean restaurant in this building?	• It's on the third floor.
• How do I get to City Hall?	• Go straight on this street for three blocks.
• Is there a coffee shop in the building?	• Please take the elevator and go up to the 7th floor.

Key Expressions

- 식당 / 체육관 / 라운지는(은) 어디 있나요?
  Where 's the restaurant / gym / lounge?
- 중식당 맛집을 추천해 주시겠습니까?
  Can you recommend a good Chinese restaurant?
- 이 빌딩에 커피숍이 있나요?
  Is there a coffee shop in the building?
- 지하에 있습니다.
  It's in the basement.
- 이 빌딩에 한식당이 어디 있나요?
  Where's the Korean restaurant in this building?
- 2개 있습니다
  There are two.
- Smith 씨 사무실이 몇 층에 있습니까?
  What floor is Mr. Smith's office on?
- 2층에 있습니다.
  It's on the second(2nd) floor.
- 엘리베이터를 타고 7층까지 올라오세요.
  Please take the elevator and go up to the 7th floor.
- 복도 끝까지 걸어가십시오.
  Walk to the end of the hallway.
- 복도를 쭉 따라가십시오.
  Go straight along this hall.
- Smith 씨 사무실이 어디인지 알려주시겠습니까?
  How can I get to Mr. Smith's office from here?
  Could you tell me where Mr. Smith's office is?
- 거기에 어떻게 가나요?
  How do I get there?
- 호텔에서 왼쪽으로 돌고 나서 직진하세요.
  Turn left at the hotel and then go straight.

- 모퉁이에 한국은행이 보일 겁니다.
  You'll see the Bank of Korea on the corner.
- 이 길로 직진하여 세 블록 가세요.
  Go straight on this street for three blocks.
- 찾기 쉬울 겁니다.
  You can't miss it.

Conversation Locations

A Excuse me. Where is the restaurant in this building?
B There are two restaurants.

A Really?
B One is Chinese and the other is Korean restaurant.

A I'm looking for a Korean restaurant.
B It's on the third floor.

A On the third floor?
B That's right.

Conversation Directions

A Can you tell me how to get to City Hall?
B City Hall? Go straight along this street and turn left at the corner, and then go up two blocks.

A Yes, I see.
B Then, you will see City Hall on your right.

A Okay. Is there some sort of a landmark you can tell me about?
B Yes, Plaza Hotel is nearby. It's across from the City Hall. You can't miss it.

A Thank you.

주요표현 연습(Pattern Drill)

1. 시청에 어떻게 가야 하는지 알려주실 수 있나요?

Can you tell me ____________ to ____________ to City Hall?

2. 이 건물에 레스토랑이 어디에 있나요?

Where are the ____________ in this ____________?

3. 호텔에서 왼쪽으로 도세요.

Turn ____________ at the ____________.

4. Smith 씨 사무실이 몇 층에 있습니까?

What ____________ is Mr. Smith's office ____________?

5. 2층에 있습니다.

__________'s ____________ the second(2nd) floor.

Unit 3

Understanding Tasks and Doing Works

Words and Phrases

- ask of you 당신에게 요청하다
- handle 다루다, 수행하다
- have it done 그것이 되다(완성되다)
- deadline 기한, 마감 시간
- turn it in ~을 제출하다
- come along (원하는 대로) 되어가다
- urgent 긴급한
- make it 해내다, 성공하다
- as soon as possible (=ASAP) 가능한 한 빨리
- right away 바로 당장
- at the latest 늦어도
- paperwork 서류작업
- in time 제 시간에
- on schedule 일정에 맞추어, 예정대로
- ahead of schedule 예정보다 빠른
- behind the schedule 예정보다 늦은
- extend 미루다, 연기하다
- complete 마치다, 완수하다

Warm up Dialogue

업무 부탁하기	응답하기
• How's the report going? • Is everything on schedule?	• I am still working on it. • It is behind the schedule. Could you extend the deadline?
• Could you do me a favor? • Please print out ten copies of this document.	• What is it? • I'll take care of it right away.

Key Expressions

〈업무 부탁 또는 지시〉

- 부탁 하나 드려도 될까요?
  Could you do me a favor?
  There's something I'd like to ask of you.
- 이 프로젝트 / 보고서에 당신의 도움이 필요해요.
  I need your help on this project.
  Would you mind helping me with the report?
- 제 보고서 좀 검토해 주시겠어요?
  Can you please review my report?
  Can you please proofread my paper?
- 당신이 할 수 있겠습니까?
  Can you handle this?
  Can you do this?

〈구체적인 데드라인 제시〉

- 기한이 언제입니까?
  When is the deadline?
  When do I need to turn it in?
- 급한 건가요?
  Is this urgent?
- 가능한 빨리해 줄 수 있습니까?
  Can you make it as soon as possible(ASAP)?
- 이건 바로 해주세요.
  This has to be done right away.
  Can you get it done right away?
- 내일까지 해주세요.
  Can you finish this by tomorrow?
  Can you get this done by tomorrow?
- 늦어도 다음 주 월요일까지는 해주세요.
  I need to have it done by next Monday at the latest.
  It should be finished by next Monday at the latest.
- 이틀 안에 끝냈으면 좋겠습니다.
  Please finish this within two days.

〈진행 상황 확인〉

- 보고서가 얼마나 진행되었습니까?
  How's the report going?
  How far are you with the report?
- (그 업무를) 다 끝내셨습니까?
  Did you get it done?
- 다 예정대로 진행되고 있습니까?
  Is everything on schedule?
- 거의 다했습니다.
  It's almost done / finished.

- 예정대로 끝날 것입니다.
  It will be done on schedule.
- 예정보다 빨리하고 있습니다.
  It is ahead of schedule.
- 예정보다 늦어지고 있습니다.
  It is behind the schedule.
- ~까지는 이 일을 마치겠습니다.
  I'll get it done by 시간 / 요일 / 날짜.
  It will be done by 시간 / 요일 / 날짜.
- 아직 하고 있는 중입니다.
  I am still working on it.
  I haven't done it yet.
- 마감 기한을 연장해 주실 수 있을까요?
  Could you extend the deadline?
- 보고서를 다음 주까지 완성해도 될까요?
  Can I complete the report by next week?
- 한 주 더 드릴 수 있어요.
  I can give you another week.
  I can give you one more week.

Conversation Understanding tasks and doing works

A Can you finish the report by 5 p.m. this afternoon? I'm going to meet the client tomorrow morning to make a presentation.
B Did you say by 5 p.m?

A Yes. Can you make it?
B I am still working on it. Can you give me more time?

A Okay, I can give you two more hours.
B Yes, It will be done in two hours. Anything else, sir?

A Please send a copy of the report in a PDF format to Mr. Lee in the Marketing Department. He also needs to review it.
B Sure. I'll send the report in a PDF file to Mr. Lee.

A Thank you.
B You're welcome, sir.

주요표현 연습(Pattern Drill)

1. 부탁 하나 드려도 될까요?

 ____________ you do me a ____________?

2. 제 보고서 좀 검토해 주시겠습니까?

 Can you please ________________ my _______________?

3. 기한이 언제입니까?

 _______________ is the ________________?

4. 가능한 빨리 해주시겠습니까?

 Can you _______________ it as _______________ as ________?

5. 예정보다 빨리 하고 있습니다.

 ____________ is _______________ of schedule.

Unit 4 Dealing with Office Equipment

Words and Phrases

- Do you know how to ~ ~할 줄 아세요?
- copy / photocopy 복사하다, 사본
- copier / photocopier 복사기
- input 입력하다
- get something fixed ~을 고치다
- be infected with a virus 바이러스에 감염되다
- install 프로그램을 깔다
- be jammed ~에 종이가 걸리다
- be out of toner 토너가 떨어지다
- access the Internet 인터넷에 접속하다
- print 인쇄하다
- scan 스캔하다
- scanner 스캐너
- document 서류
- file 파일, 서류철
- recycling paper 이면지
- enlarge 확대하다
- reduce 축소하다
- work 작동하다
- out of order 고장난

Warm up Dialogue

사무기기 사용 요청하기	응답하기
• Do you know how to use this copier?	• Yes, I do. How many copies do you want?
• The copier doesn't work.	• It's jammed.
• I can't access the Internet.	• The computer is infected with a virus.
• How many copies do you want?	• Print the document, and make five copies of it.

Key Expressions

- 복사기 사용할 줄 아세요?
  Do you know how to use this copier?
- 문서를 인쇄해서 5부 복사해 주세요.
  Print the document, and make five copies of it.
- 몇 부를 복사할까요?
  How many copies do you need?
- 3부 단면 복사 부탁해요.
  Please make three single sided.
- 양면 복사를 할 수 있나요?
  Can I make copies double sided?
- A3로 확대해 주세요.
  Please enlarge this to A3.
- A4로 축소해 주세요.
  Please reduce this to A4.
- 복사기에 용지가 떨어졌어요.
  The copying machine is out of paper.
- 인쇄용 종이가 좀 필요합니다.
  I need some paper for the printer.
- 복사기에 종이가 걸렸어요.
  The copy machine is jammed.
  It's jammed.
- 복사기가 고장 난 것 같아요.
  The copier doesn't work.
  The copier seems to be out of order.
- 회의록 좀 인쇄해 주시겠습니까?
  Will you print out the minutes of the meeting?
- 파일 이름을 뭐라고 저장했죠?
  What did you name the file?
- 컴퓨터가 바이러스에 감염되었어요.
  The computer is infected with a virus.
- 와이파이에 어떻게 접속하죠?
  How do I get on the WIFI?
- 이곳 와이파이 아이디와 비밀번호가 무엇입니까?
  What is the Wi-Fi ID and password here?
- 인터넷에 어떻게 접속하죠?
  How do I get on the internet?
- 인터넷에 접속이 안 돼요.
  I can't access the Internet.
- 인터넷이 너무 느려요.
  The Internet is very slow.
- Dr. Davis께 오후에 이메일을 보내겠습니다.
  I'll send an email to Dr. Davis this afternoon.
  I'll send it to Dr. Davis by email this afternoon.
- 요청하신 자료를 보냅니다.
  I'm sending you the documents you're requested.
- 첨부파일을 확인해 주시기 바랍니다.
  Please check the attachments.

Conversation Dealing with office equipment

A Sandra, I have to make copies, but this copier seems to be out of order.
B Really? Let me see. Hmm... It's jammed!

A Sorry, but I don't know how to fix it.
B It's Okay. I can do it for you. How many copies do you want?

A Three.
B Do you want it double sided?

A Yes, please. Thank you for your help.
B No trouble.

주요표현 연습(Pattern Drill)

1. 인터넷에 접속이 안 돼요.

   I can't ______________ the ______________.

2. 복사기 사용할 줄 아세요?

   Do you know ________ ______ use this ______________?

3. 몇 부 복사할까요?

   How ______________ copies do you ______________?

4. 복사기에 종이가 걸렸어요.

   It's ______________________.

5. 복사기가 고장 났어요.

   The copier is __________ of ______________.

Grammar Point

❶ 위치전치사(Prepositions of Location)

in	~(안)에	The ball is in the box.
on	~위에 (~에 붙어서)	The ball is on the box.
over	~위에 (~에서 떨어져서 바로)	The ball is over the box.
under	~아래에 (~에서 떨어져서 바로)	The ball is under the box.
above	~(부다) 위에, ~위쪽에	The ball is above the box.
below	~(보다) 아래에, ~아래쪽에	The ball is below the box.
in front of	~앞에	The ball is in front of the box.
behind	~뒤에	The ball is behind the box.
by, next to, beside, near	~옆에	The ball is next to the box.

(위치) 전치사 개념도

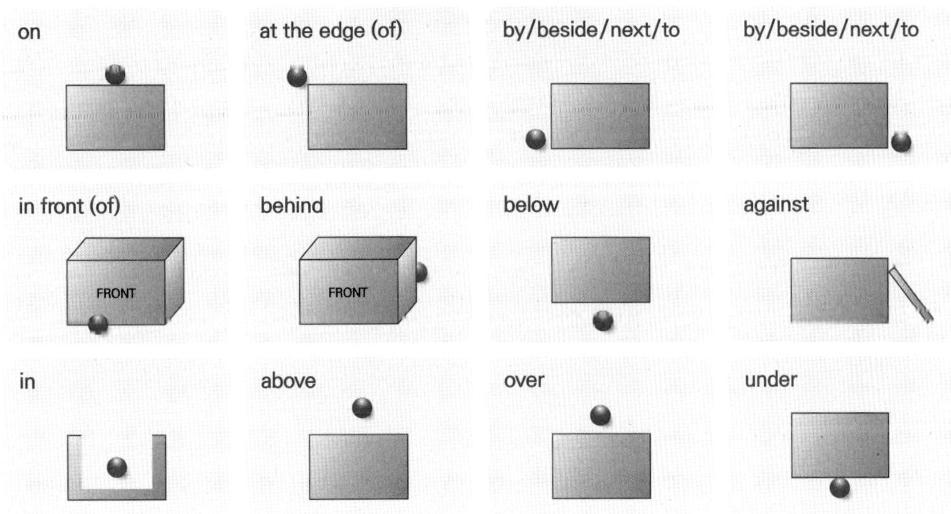

❷ 방향과 움직임을 나타내는 전치사

up	~위쪽으로	He is going up the stairs.
down	~아래쪽으로	He is coming down the stairs.
into	~안으로	He came into the room.
out of	~밖으로	He went out of the room.
along	~을 따라서	He walked along the street.
across	~을 건너	He walked across the street.
through	~을 통해	He came into the room through the door.
to	~에, ~으로	He went to the post office.
toward, towards	~쪽으로	He went toward (= towards) the post office.
between	~사이에 (둘)	The ball is between two boxes.

(움직임) 전치사 개념도

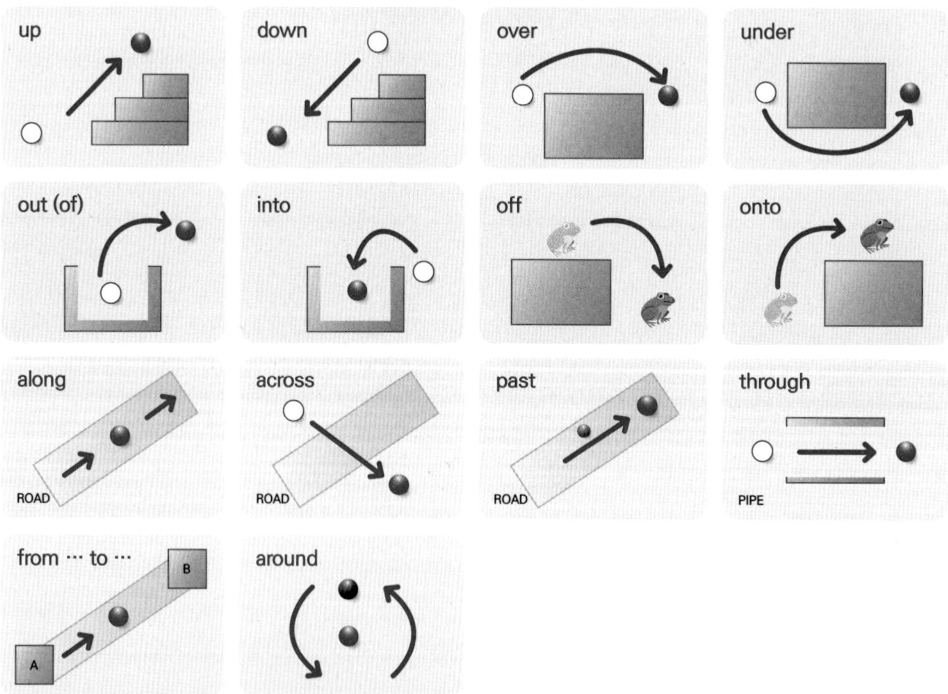

Practicing on Your Own

Look at the site map and complete the sentences using page 43 & 44 diagrams. (지도를 보고 방향 전치사를 이용해 문장을 완성하세요)

a. Information Center is __________________ the main gate.

b. Rest Room is __________ Gift Shop ______ Drug Store.

c. Snack Bar is __________ Office Supplies.

d. Drug Store is ____________ the main gate.

e. ABC Company is _________ Office Supplies.

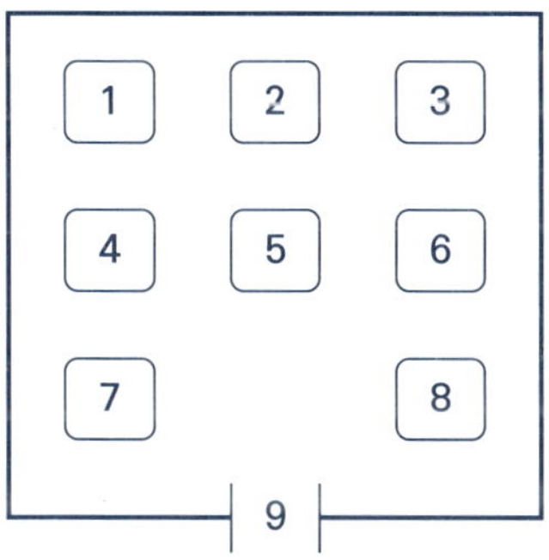

1 Snack Bar
2 Office Supplies
3 Gift Shop
4 Restaurant
5 ABC Company
6 Rest Room
7 Information center
8 Drug Store
9 Main Gate

Language Check

Match the meanings of the phrases in bold letters to the explanations on the right side. (굵은 글씨로 된 구절의 의미와 같은 단어를 연결하세요)

1. **to take someone into a vehicle** • • a. basement

2. The coffee shop is **opposite side of our building.** • • b. pick up

3. He is standing **ahead of** me. • • c. across from

4. the floor of a building **underground** • • d. in front of

Work in pairs

Practice with your classmates. Give a responses to these requests. (A가 요청한 것에 대해 답을 하는 상황입니다. 대화를 연습해보세요)

Speaker A Can you send an email?
type this report?
copy these documents?
file these papers?

Speaker B Yes, of course.
No problem.
I'll be happy to help.
All right. I will do it for you.

업무에서 다루는 문서 용어

한글 명칭	영어 명칭
사업계획서	business plan
주간 보고서	weekly report
월간 보고서	monthly report
연간 보고서	annual report
영업보고서	sales report
시장 조사 보고서	market research report
제안서	proposal
계약서	contract
견적서	quotation
명세서	statement
송장	invoice
원고, 초안	draft
회의록	minutes

Chapter 03

Business Telephoning

Unit 1 Making & Receiving a Call

Words and Phrases

- speak to / talk to ~와 통화하다
- extension(number) 내선번호
- country code / national code 국가 번호
- local code / area code 지역번호
- cell phone / mobile phone number 휴대폰 번호
- conference call 전화 회의
- make a call 전화 걸다
- take a call / receive a call 전화 받다
- local call 시내 전화
- long-distance call 장거리 전화
- international call 국제 전화
- pick up the phone 수화기를 들다
- answer the phone 전화를 받다
- on behalf of ~를 대신하여

Warm up Dialogue 1

전화 걸기	응답하기
• May I speak to Mr. Larry Smith, please?	• This is Larry Smith speaking.
• Good morning. ABC Company. How may I help you?	• Good morning. This is Gina Kim from SNH Company. I'd like to speak to Mr. Paul Kim.
• Can I speak to Mr. Kim?	• Hold on, please. I'll see if he is available.

Key Expressions

<전화 걸기>

- Mr. Smith와 통화할 수 있을까요?
  May I speak to Mr. Smith, please?
  Can I speak to Mr. Smith, please?
- 매니저와 통화하고 싶습니다.
  I'd like to speak with the manager, please.
- 회계부서의 Mr. Paul Kim과 통화하고 싶습니다.
  I'd like to speak to Mr. Paul Kim in the Accounting Department.
- 영업부서(내선번호 212번)를 연결해 주시겠습니까?
  Could you put me through to the Sales Department(Ext. 212)?
- 제 전화를 기다리고 계십니다. Paul Kim이라고 전해주세요.
  He is expecting my call. Tell him it's Paul Kim calling.
- 저는 Mr. Smith를 대신하여 전화드렸습니다.
  I'm calling on behalf of Mr. Smith.

<전화 받기>

- 저는 ABC 회사의 Paul Kim입니다. 무엇을 도와드릴까요?
  This is Paul Kim from ABC Company. May I help you?
- Paul Kim입니다.
  This is Paul Kim speaking.
- 제가 바로 그 사람입니다.
  This is he / she speaking.

Conversation Making a call

A Good morning. Cheil Electonics, may I help you?
B Good morning. May I speak to Ms. Nancy Hamilton, please?

A Can I ask who's calling, please?
B This is Paul Kim from ABC Company.

A Hold on, please. I'll transfer your call to Ms. Hamilton now.
B Thank you.

Warm up Dialogue 2

전화 건 목적 말하기	응답하기
• I'm calling to arrange an appointment with Mr. Kim. • This is Gina Kim from SNH Company. I'm calling to schedule a meeting to discuss the project.	• Certainly. Could you tell me your name, please? • Just a moment, please. I'll transfer your call to Ms. Brown. She is in charge of the project.

Key Expressions

〈전화 건 목적 말하기〉

- Mr. Kim과 약속을 정하려고 전화드렸습니다.
  I calling to arrange an appointment with Mr. Kim.
- 화요일 회의 확인 차 전화드렸습니다.
  I'm calling to confirm Tuesday's meeting.
- 9월 20일 미팅 건으로 전화드렸습니다.
  I'm calling about our meeting on September 20th.
- 프로젝트에 관한 회의를 잡았으면 해서 전화드렸습니다.
  I'm calling to schedule a meeting to discuss the project.
- 뉴욕 출장 건으로 전화드렸습니다.
  I'm calling about a business trip to New York.

Conversation Stating the purpose of the call

A Good morning. Sun Industries, may I help you?
B Good morning. This is Nancy Hamilton. Can I speak to Mr. Chris Lee, please?

A This is Chris Lee speaking. How are you, Ms. Hamilton?
B Great, thanks. And you?

A Doing well, thank you.
B I'm calling to see if we can schedule a meeting to discuss our project.

A Sure. When would be most convenient for you?
B Can we meet next Monday?

A Yes, that works. What time would be best for you?
B How about 10:00 in the morning?

A Sounds good. I'm looking forward to meeting you.
B Likewise. I'll see you next Monday at 10 a.m.

A Good bye.
B Bye now.

주요표현 연습(Pattern Drill)

1. 저는 SNH사의 Gina Kim입니다. 무엇을 도와드릴까요?

   ________ is Gina Kim ________ SNH Company. ________ I ________ you?

2. Mr. Chris Lee와 통화할 수 있을까요?

   ________ I ________ to Mr. Chris Lee, please?

3. 제가 Chris Lee입니다.

   ________ ________ Chris Lee ________.

4. 영업부의 Mr. Smith와 통화하고 싶습니다.

   I'd like to ________ ________ Mr. Smith in the ________ Department.

5. 화요일 회의 확인 차 전화드렸습니다.

   I'm calling to ________ Tuesday's ________.

Unit 2

Transferring a Call

Words and Phrases

- hold on (전화를) 끊지 않고 잠시 기다리다
- transfer a call / connect a call 전화를 연결하다
- put A through to B A의 전화를 B에게 연결하다
- busy signal 통화 중 신호
- available 가능한
- free 한가한
- in regard to ~에 관하여
- put someone on hold ~를 대기시키다

Warm up Dialogue

전화 연결 요청하기	응답하기
• May I ask who's calling?	• This is Paul Kim from ABC Company.
• May I ask what this is in regard to?	• I'd like to talk about the project meeting next week.
• Could you put me through to the Sales Department extension 212?	• I'm sorry, that line's busy. Will you hold?

Key Expressions

- 어느 분을 찾으십니까?
  Who would you like to talk to?
  Who are you trying to reach?

- 실례지만 누구시라고 전해드릴까요?
  May I ask who's calling?
  Can I ask who's calling?

- 성함을 말씀해 주시겠습니까?
  Can I have your name, please?

- 무슨 용건입니까?
  May I ask what this is in regard to?
  Can I ask what this is about?

- 이 전화를 Mr. Smith 씨 사무실로 돌려주시겠습니까?
  Would you transfer this call to Mr. Smith's office?

<통화 대기>

- 잠시만 기다려주세요.
  One moment, please.
  Just a moment, please.

- 끊지 말고 잠시 기다려주시기 바랍니다 .
  Hold the line, please.
  May I put you on hold?

- 잠시만 기다려주세요. 그가 가능한지 알아보겠습니다.
  Hold on, please. I'll see if he's free.
  Hold on, please. I'll see it he's available.

- 죄송하지만 통화 중입니다. 끊지 말고 기다려 주시겠습니까?
  I'm sorry, that line's busy. Will you hold?
  I'm sorry, that line's engaged. Will you hold?

<전화 연결>

- Mr. Kim께 연결해 드리겠습니다.
  I'll put you through to Mr. Kim.
  I'll transfer you to Mr. Kim.
  I'll connect you to Mr. Kim.

- 연결되었습니다.
  You're through.

Conversation Transferring a call

A Good morning. SNH company, may I help you?
B Good morning. I'd like to speak to Ms. Gina Kim, please.

A One moment, please. I'll put you through. (after a few minutes) I'm afraid Ms. Kim is not in the office right now. Would you like to leave a message?
B No, thanks. When do you expect her to be back?

A She should be back by 2 o'clock this afternoon.
B Okay, thank you. I'll call back later then.

주요표현 연습(Pattern Drill)

1. 실례지만 누구라고 전해드릴까요?

__________ I ask __________________ calling?

2. 무슨 용건인가요?

May I ask _____________ this is in _____________________ to?

3. 죄송하지만 통화 중입니다.

I'm _______________, that line's ____________________.

4. 끊지 말고 잠시만 기다려주세요.

_____________ the line, please.

5. Mr. Kim께 연결해 드리겠습니다.

I'll __________ you __________________ to Mr. Kim.

Unit 3

Unable to Answer a Call

Words and Phrases

- conference / meeting 회의
- business trip 출장
- out of the office 부재중
- out for lunch 점심 식사하러 나가다
  (breakfast 아침식사, dinner 저녁식사, brunch 점심 겸 늦은 아침식사)
- step out / step away 나가다, 자리를 비우다
- client / customer 고객
- visitor 방문객
- expect 예상하다
- take a day off 하루 휴무를 내다
- on vacation 휴가 중
- call in sick 병가를 내다

Warm up Dialogue

전화 통화 요청하기	응답하기
• May I speak to Mr. Larry Smith?	• Mr. Smith is on the phone at the moment.
• I'd like to speak with the Sales manager, please.	• I'm sorry, but he's with a client now.
• Can I speak to Ms. Gina Kim?	• I'm sorry, but she's on a business trip.
• When do you expect her to be back?	• She will be back next Friday.

Key Expressions

- Mr. Smith는 통화 중입니다.
  Mr. Smith is on the phone at the moment.
  Mr. Smith is on the other line.
- 회의 중입니다.
  He's in a meeting now.
  He's in a conference now.
- 고객 / 방문객과 함께 계십니다.
  He's with a client.
  He's with a customer.
  He's with a visitor.
- 지금 사무실에 안 계십니다.
  She is out of the office.
  She is not in the office.
- 방금 자리를 비우셨습니다.
  He just stepped away from his desk.
  He just stepped out from his desk.
  He is not at the desk at the moment.
- 점심식사 중입니다.
  He's out for lunch.
  He's at lunch.
- 오늘 조퇴하셨습니다.
  He left early today.
- 오늘 하루 휴무입니다.
  He took a day off today.
- 오늘 하루 병가 내셨습니다.
  He called in sick today.
- 퇴근하셨습니다.
  He has gone for the day.
- 출장 중입니다.
  He's on a business trip.
- 휴가 중으로 며칠간 안 계십니다.
  He's on vacation, and he'll be off for a couple of days.
- 언제쯤 돌아오십니까?
  When do you expect him to be back?
- 금요일에 돌아오십니다.
  He'll be back on Friday.
  He won't be back until Friday.

Conversation Unable to answer a call

A Hello, SNH Company. May I help you?
B Hello, may I speak to Ms. Gina Kim, please?

A May I ask what you're calling for?
B I'm returning Ms. Kim's call.

A I see. I apologize but she took a day off today. Would you like to leave her a message?
B That's all right. I'll call her back tomorrow.

A Thank you. Good bye.
B Good bye.

주요표현 연습(Pattern Drill)

1. Mr. Kim은 통화 중입니다.

Mr. Kim is on the __________ __________.

Mr. Kim은 지금 회의 중입니다.

Mr. Kim is __________ a __________ now.

2. 그는 점심식사 중입니다.

He's __________ for __________.

그는 오늘 휴무입니다.

He __________ a __________ off today.

3. 그는 방금 자리를 비우셨습니다.

He just __________ away __________ his desk.

그녀는 지금 사무실에 안 계십니다.

She is __________ __________ the office.

4. 그는 출장 중입니다.

He's ___________ a business ___________.

휴가 중으로 며칠간 안 계십니다.

He's on ___________, and he'll be ___________ for a couple of days.

5. 그는 언제 돌아오십니까?

___________ do you ___________ him to be back?

금요일에 돌아오십니다.

He will be ______________ ___________ Friday.

Unit 4

Leaving & Taking a Message

Words and Phrases

- call back / return one's call 회신 전화하다
- leave a message 메시지를 남기다
- take a message 메시지를 받다
- as soon as possible(ASAP) 가능한 한 빨리
- convenient 편리한
- inconvenient 불편한
- double-check 재확인하다
- read back (확인을 위하여) 다시 읽다
- contact number 연락처
- repeat 반복하다
- spell 철자를 말하다
- confirm 확인하다
- get back to someone ~에게 다시 연락하다
- arrange an appointment 약속을 정하다
- schedule a meeting 회의 일정을 잡다
- in charge of ~를 담당하고 있는, ~를 책임지고 있는

Warm up Dialogue

메시지 남기기	응답하기
• Would you like to leave a message?	• Please ask him to call me as soon as possible.
• May I take a message?	• Could you ask him to call me back?
• Can I have your name and contact number?	• Sure. My name is Gina Kim, and contact number is 010-5555-7319.

Key Expressions

- 메시지를 남기겠습니까?
  Would you like to leave a message?
- 제가 메시지를 받아도 될까요?
  May I take a message?
  Can I give him / her a message for you?
- 메시지를 전해드리겠습니다.
  I'll give him the message.
  I'll pass this along to Mr. Smith.
- (그에게 / 그녀에게) 메시지를 확실하게 전달하겠습니다.
  I'll make sure that she / he gets the message.
- 성함과 연락처를 알려주시겠습니까?
  Can I have your name and contact number?
- 성함 철자를 알려주시겠습니까?
  Could you spell your name, please?
- 전화 좀 부탁합니다.
  Could you ask him to call me back?
- 가능한 한 빨리 전화해 달라고 전해주세요.
  Please ask him to call me as soon as possible.
- 그가 들어오는 대로 전화드리라고 전하겠습니다.
  I'll have him call you back as soon as he gets in.
- 02-123-4567번으로 전화 부탁한다고 전해주세요.
  Please ask him to call me at 02-123-4567.

Conversation Leaving & Taking a message

A Good morning. P&B Associations. How can I help you?
B I'd like to speak to Mr. Larry Smith, please.

A May I ask who's calling, please?
B This is Nancy Hamilton from Cheil Electronics.

A One minute, please. I'll see if Mr. Smith is available right now.
B Great, thank you.

A I apologize but he's currently in a meeting and is unavailable right now. May I take a message?
B Sure, please ask him to call me back. This is about the project meeting next week.

A Certainly. I'll make sure that he gets the message. May I have your number just in case?

B Sure. My number is 02-357-7799.

A And could you spell your last name, please?

B It's H-A-M-I-L-T-O-N.

A All right, Ms. Hamilton. I'll pass this along to Mr. Smith.

B Thank you. Good bye.

A Good bye.

주요표현 연습(Pattern Drill)

1. 메시지를 남기시겠습니까?

______________ you like to ______________ a message?

2. 메시지를 전해드리겠습니다.

I'll ______________ him the ______________.

3. 성함과 연락처를 알려주시겠습니까?

Can I ______________ your ______________ and contact number?

4. 가능한 한 빨리 전화달라고 해주세요.

Please ______________ him to ______________ me as soon as possible.

5. 010-123-4567번으로 전화 부탁한다고 전해주세요.

Please ______________ her to call me ______________ 010-123-4567.

Important
message

메시지를 받을 사람	For ________
메시지를 남긴 사람	From ________
전화 받은 시간과 날짜	Time ________ Date ________
메시지를 남긴 사람의 전화번호	Phone ________
긴급한 전화인 경우 체크	URGENT ________
전달 메시지	Message ________

Unit 5

Wrong Calls & Problems with Calls

Words and Phrases

- wrong 틀린, 잘못된
- dial incorrectly 전화를 잘못 걸다
- redial 전화를 다시 걸다
- speak up 크게 말하다
- connection 연결
- be crossed 혼선되다
- out of order 고장나다
- run out of ~을 소진하다
- hang up the phone 전화를 끊다
- crack 금이 가다, 깨진
- mute 음소거하다

Warm up Dialogue

통화 중 문제 발생	해결하기
• Hello. Can I speak to Mr. Paul Kim, please?	• I'm sorry I can't hear you. Can you speak up a bit?
• Hello. Is this 02-345-7890?	• I'm sorry, but you must have the wrong number.
• Can I speak to Dr. Davis?	• I'm sorry, but it's a bad connection. Could you call again?

Key Expressions

- 전화 잘못 거셨습니다.
  I'm sorry you've got the wrong number.
  You must have the wrong number.
- 죄송하지만 그런 이름을 가진 분은 안 계십니다.
  I'm sorry there is no one by that name.
  I'm sorry there is no one with that name.
- 번호는 맞지만 미스터 김이라고 불리는 분은 안 계십니다.
  The number is correct, but there is no one called Mr. Kim here.
- 지금 거신 번호는 567-1233으로 변경되었습니다.
  The number you have dialed has been changed to 567-1233.
- 잘 들리지 않습니다.
  I'm sorry I can't hear you.
  I can hardly hear you.
- 연결상태가 좋지 않습니다. 제가 다시 걸겠습니다.
  It's a bad connection. Let me call you again.
- 전화를 끊고 다시 걸어주시겠습니까?
  Could you hang up and call again?
- 조금 크게 말씀해 주시겠습니까?
  I'm sorry, but could you speak up a bit, please?
  I'm sorry, but could you speak a little louder, please?
- 조금 천천히 말씀해 주시겠습니까?
  I'm sorry, but could you speak more slowly, please?
- 죄송하지만 다시 말씀해 주시겠습니까?
  I'm sorry, but could you repeat that, please?
- 혼선되었습니다. 다시 전화 주시겠습니까?
  The lines are crossed. Can you call again, please?
- 배터리가 거의 다 소모되었습니다.
  My battery is almost dead.
  My battery is running out.
- 제 전화가 고장 났습니다.
  My phone is not working.
  My phone is out of order.
- 휴대폰 전원이 꺼졌어요.
  My phone is dead.
- 휴대폰 화면 액정에 금이 갔어요.
  The display screen on my cell phone is cracked.
- 핸드폰을 무음으로 해주세요.
  You should put your cell phone on mute.

Conversation Wrong calls

A ABC Company, may I help you?

B Hello, can I speak to James Stewart, please?

A I'm sorry, but who would you like to talk to?

B James Stewart .

A I'm sorry, but you must have the wrong number. There is no one here by that name.

B Oh, I'm so sorry.

A No worries.

Conversation Problem with calls

A ABC Company, may I help you?

B Hello, can I speak to Mr. Paul Kim?

A I'm sorry, I can't hear you very well. Could you speak up a bit, please?

B Sure, can you hear me now?

A Yes, that's much better. Thank you.

주요표현 연습(Pattern Drill)

1. 전화 잘못 거셨습니다.

   You must ______________ the ______________ number.

2. 여기 그런 이름을 가진 분은 안 계십니다.

   I'm sorry ______________ is no ______________ here by that name.

3. 어느 분을 찾으십니까?

   ______________ would you ______________ to talk to?

4. 잘 들리지 않습니다. 조금 크게 말씀해 주시겠습니까?

I'm sorry I can't ____________ you. Could you ____________ ____________ a bit, please?

5. 배터리가 거의 다 소모되었습니다.

My ______________ is almost ______________.

자동 응답기(Answering Machine)

1. Answering Machine

You have reached Human Net's Customer Service Center. We're sorry, but we can't answer the phone right now. Please leave a message after the tone and we'll get back to you as soon as we can.

휴먼넷의 고객 서비스 센터입니다. 죄송하지만 지금은 전화를 받을 수 없습니다. 신호음 후 메시지를 남겨 주시면 최대한 빨리 연락드리겠습니다.

2. Caller

Hello. This is Gina Kim. I'm calling regarding my special order. My phone number is 02-123-4567. Would you please call me before noon tomorrow?

안녕하세요. 김지나입니다. 특별 주문 건으로 전화드렸습니다. 제 전화번호는 02-123-4567입니다. 내일 정오 전에 전화 주시겠습니까?

비즈니스 전화 Tips(Business Telephone Call Planning Tips)

전화 걸기(Making Productive Telephone Calls)

1. 통화 전: 의제나 안건에 대한 미니 목록을 작성하여 메모하기
2. 통화 시작
   - 인사말을 하고 자신을 명확하게 밝힘
   - 전화를 건 이유를 제시
3. 통화 중
   - 긍정적인 전화 분위기 조성
   - 목표를 명확하게 전달
4. 통화 종료
   - 통회 결과를 확인

정중한 마무리 인사말

예) Thank you for your help. I've enjoyed talking with you. Have a good day.

전화 받기(Receiving Calls)

1. 통화 시작: 인사말과 본인 이름, 직위, 회사이름을 명확하게 밝힘
2. 통화 중: 또렷한 목소리로 통화
3. 통화 종료: 책임감 있고 도움이 될 수 있도록 응답

친절한 마무리 인사말

예) Thank you for calling.
Nice talking to you.
Have a good day.

영어로 배워보는 부서 / 직함

부서명	영문 부서명
총무부	General Affairs Department
재무부	Finance Department
인사부	Human Resources Department
영업부	Sales Department
구매부	Purchasing Department
마케팅부	Marketing Department
생산부	Production Department
연구개발부	Research and Development Department
소비자서비스부	Customer Service Department
회계부	Accounting Department

직함	영문 직함
회장	Chairperson
사장 부사장	President Vice President
최고경영자 최고재무관리자 마케팅총괄이사 최고운영책임자 최고전략책임자 최고기술경영자 최고디지털책임자	CEO (Chief Executive Officer) CFO (Chief Financial Officer) CMO (Chief Marketing Officer) COO (Chief Operating Officer) CSO (Chief Strategy Officer) CTO (Chief Technology Officer) CDO (Chief Digital Officer)
전무이사 상무이사 이사	Senior Managing Director Managing Director Director
부장	General Manager
차장	Sub-manager, Deputy General Manager
과장	Manager
대리	Assistant Manager
*지점장	Branch Manager

Grammar Point

❶ 시간전치사(Prepositions of Time)

on: days & dates (요일이나 날짜 앞에 옴)

Ex. on Sunday, on July 4th

in: months & years, seasons, part of the day (월, 연도, 계절, 하루의 일부분 앞에 옴)

Ex. in May, in 2020, in Spring, in the morning, in the afternoon, in the evening

at: specific time or specific of day (특정한 시간 또는 하루의 특정 시간대 앞에 옴)

Ex. at 8 o'clock, at night, at dawn, at midnight

❷ 시간, 요일, 월, 휴일 표기

오전(A.M.) 또는 오후(P.M.)와 함께 쓰이는 시간은 숫자로 표기한다.

시간과 분을 표기할 때는 시:분(ex. 1:30 p.m.), 시간만 표기할 때는 :00을 생략한다.(ex. 9 a.m.)

요일, 월, 휴일은 항상 대문자를 사용한다.

Ex. Monday, Wednesday, January, April, New Year's Day, Christmas

❸ 기간을 나타내는 시간 전치사: by, until, in, for

Ex. I'll be away until next week.

I'm away for a week.

I should be back by the end of the week.

I'll be back in two days.

Practicing on Your Own

Ⓐ Complete the following sentences with the correct prepositions. (알맞은 전치사를 이용하여 문장을 완성하세요)

1. I'll see you ______ three o'clock.

2. I'll see you ______ Wednesday.

3. I can make it ______ the morning.

4. I can't make it ______ Monday afternoon.

5. I can't make it ______ September 2nd.

6. We can meet ______ May.

7. I can't make it ______ 3:30 p.m.

8. Can you make it ______ the evening?

9. No, but I'm free ______ the morning.

B **Write the questions out correctly.** (괄호 안의 단어를 이용하여 의문문을 만드세요)

Ex. (calling / who / is?)

Who's calling? / It's John.

1. (speak / who / did / to / you?)

______________________________ / I spoke to the department manager.

2. (this evening / coming / who / is?)

______________________________ / Just our two Japanese agents.

3. (left / who / briefcase / a / here / yesterday?)

______________________________ / I did.

4. (is / boss / your / who?)

______________________________ / Kathrin Mathys.

5. (you / report / do / who / to?)

______________________________ / I report to Kathrin Mathys.

C In the following conversation , choose the most suitable response. (다음 전화대화에서 밑줄 친 표현 중 알맞은 것을 고르세요)

A Hello, is that accounts?

B Yes, **it is. / I am.**

A I'd like to speak to Sara Adams, please.

B **I am / This is** Sara Adams.

A Hello, my name is Jessica Brown from ABC Company. **I call / I'm calling** about a bill we sent you.

B Oh, you should speak to my colleague, Roger Simons. I'll put you through to his extension.

A Thank you.

B The line's busy. **Are you holding? / Will you hold?**

A Yes, **I am / I will.**

B I'm afraid the line is still busy. **Would / Could** you give me your number and **I / I'll** ask him to call you **again / back?**

A Yes, certainly. It's 568-9839.

B Thank you. Goodbye.

A Goodbye.

Language Check

A Match the verbs with the objects. (복적어와 농사를 연결하세요)

1. to dial • • a. a phone
2. to make • • b. a message
3. to leave • • c. a number
4. to use • • d. a call

B **Match the meanings of the phrases in bold letters to the explanations on the right side.** (굵은 글씨로 쓰인 문장의 뜻을 오른쪽 알맞은 표현과 연결하세요)

1. **Who's calling** please? •	• a. busy
2. I'll just **put you through**. •	• b. wait (on the phone)
3. Would you like to **hold**? •	• c. come to
4. I can't **make** the meeting next Monday. •	• d. make the connection for you
5. I'm **tied up** all day. •	• e. What's your name?

Chapter 04

Meeting Arrangement

Unit 1

Arranging a Meeting

Words and Phrases

- make / set up an appointment 약속을 정하다, 약속을 잡다
- arrange a meeting 회의를 준비하다
- set a date 날짜를 정하다
- schedule 일정, 스케줄
- be scheduled to / be arranged to ~하기로 예정되어 있다
- check the schedule / check the calendar 일정을 확인하다
- make / have a meeting 회의를 하다
- available 가능한
- convenient 편리한
- previous appointment / prior engagement 선약
- be tied up 너무 바빠 꼼짝 못하다, ~에 묶이다
- fully booked 일정이 꽉 차있는
- all day 하루 종일
- look forward to+동사원형+ing ~하기를 고대하다
- several matters 몇 가지 건(문제)

Warm up Dialogue

미팅 약속 요청하기	응답하기
• Can we schedule a meeting now? • I'm calling to set a date for our next meeting.	• Let me look at my schedule. • What date would be best for you?
• Are you available next Monday? • How about Friday?	• I'm afraid I have a previous appointment then. • I'm afraid I can't make it that day.

Key Expressions

- 미팅 약속을 정하고 싶습니다.
  I'd like to make an appointment for a meeting.
  Could we set up a meeting schedule now?
- Mr. Smith 씨와 미팅 약속을 잡으려고 전화드렸습니다.
  I'm calling to schedule a meeting with Mr. Smith.
- 다음 회의 날짜를 정하기 위하여 전화드렸습니다.
  I'm calling to set a date for our next meeting.
- 제 일정을 한번 살펴보겠습니다.
  Let me check my calendar.
  Let me look at my schedule.
- 목요일에 뵐 수 있을까요?
  Can we make it on Thursday?
  Can we make the meeting on Thursday?
- 언제 만나 뵐까요?
  When do you like to meet?
  What day would be best for you?
- 몇 시에 만나 뵐까요?
  What time shall we meet?
- 죄송하지만 선약이 있습니다.
  I'm afraid I have a previous appointment then.
  Actually, I have another appointment then.
- 죄송하지만 내일은 일정이 꽉 차 있습니다.
  I'm afraid I'm tied up tomorrow.
- 죄송하지만 안 될 것 같습니다. 이번 주에 출장을 가야 합니다.
  I'm afraid I can't make it because I have to go on a business trip.
- 죄송하지만 다음 주 금요일까지는 안 될 것 같습니다.
  I'm afraid I can't make it until next Friday.
- 죄송하지만 하루 종일 외근입니다.
  I'm sorry. I'm out all day.
- 금요일 오전 11시는 어떨까요?
  How about Friday at 11 a.m.?
- 금요일 좋습니다. / 좋습니다.
  Friday would be fine.
  Sure, that's fine.
- 그때 뵙겠습니다.
  I'll see you then.
  I look forward to seeing you then.

Conversation Arranging a meeting

A Sun Industries, may I help you?
B Hello, this is Jessica Brown from ABC Company.

A Hello! This is Chris Lee speaking. How are you, Jessica?
B Very well, and you?

A Likewise, thank you.
B I'm calling to see if we can arrange a meeting. There are several matters I'd like to discuss with you.

A Sure, when would be convenient for you?
B Can we meet tomorrow?

A Yes, I'm available. What time would be best for you?
B How about 3 p.m.?

A Great, that works.
B So, we'll meet you at your office at 3 p.m. tomorrow, right?

A Right. See you then.
B See you tomorrow.

주요표현 연습(Pattern Drill)

1. 미팅 약속을 정하고 싶습니다.

I'd like to ____________ an appointment for a ____________.

2. 죄송하지만 이번 주에 출장을 가야 합니다.

I'm sorry I have to ________ on a ______________________ trip.

3. 제 일정을 한번 살펴보겠습니다.

____________ me ______________ my calendar.

4. 죄송하지만 내일은 일정이 꽉 차 있습니다.

I'm afraid I'm ____________ ___________ tomorrow.

5. 그때 뵙겠습니다.

I _________________ forward to _________________ you then.

Unit 2

Confirming a Meeting

Words and Phrases

- confirm 확인하다
- confirm a meeting 회의를 확인하다
- confirm an appointment 약속을 확인하다
- check the time 시간을 확인하다
- make sure of ~을 확인하다(확실하게 하다)
- meeting place 미팅 장소
- at my office / at your office 제 사무실에서 / 당신 사무실에서
- leave him / her a message 그 / 그녀에게 메시지를 남기다

Warm up Dialogue

일정 확인 요청하기	응답하기
• I'm calling to confirm Tuesday's meeting.	• Can I check the time?
• How about Tuesday at 1 p.m.?	• Great. Do you know where the meeting place is?
• It's at my office, isn't it?	• That's right. I'll see you on Tuesday at 1 p.m. at your office.
• Good bye.	• Good bye.

Key Expressions

- 화요일 미팅 확인 차 전화 드렸습니다.
  I'm calling to confirm Tuesday's meeting.
- 화요일 미팅 확인 차 이메일드렸습니다.
  This email is to confirm Tuesday's meeting.
- 월요일 괜찮으십니까?
  Are you still OK for Monday?
- 시간을 확인해도 될까요?
  Can I check the time?
  I just wanted to make sure of the time.
- 미팅 장소를 아십니까?
  Do you know where the meeting place is?
  I just wanted to make sure of the meeting place.
- 제 사무실에서 내일 오후 4시에 만나기로 약속되어 있습니다.
  We're scheduled to meet at 4 p.m. tomorrow at my office.
- 일정표에 회의가 잡혀 있습니다.
  I have scheduled the meeting on my calendar.
- 약속 확인 차 전화하셨다고 메시지를 남겨드리겠습니다.
  I'll leave him a message that you called to confirm the appointment.

Conversation Confirming a meeting

A Good morning, Gina Kim from SNI I Company speaking.

B Hello, Gina. This is Chris Lee from Sun Industries.

A Oh, hello, Chris.

B I'm calling to confirm the meeting with Ms. Helen Oh. It is scheduled for Tuesday at 10 a.m. at her office.

A Yes, I see that Ms. Oh has it scheduled on her calendar. I'll leave her a message that you called to confirm tomorrow's meeting.

B Thank you very much.

주요표현 연습(Pattern Drill)

1. Ms. Helen Oh와 미팅 확인 차 전화드렸습니다.

   I'm calling to ____________ my meeting ______________ Ms. Helen Oh.

2. 당신 사무실에서 화요일 오전 10시에 만나기로 약속되어 있습니다.

   It is _______________ for Tuesday _________ 10 a.m. ________ your office.

3. 시간을 확인해도 될까요?

   Can I _____________ the time?

4. 회의 장소를 아십니까?

   Do you know _____________ the _____________ place is?

5. 내일 미팅 확인 차 전화하셨다고 메시지를 남겨드리겠습니다.

   I'll _____________ her a message that you called to confirm _____________ meeting.

Unit 3

Changing a Meeting

Words and Phrases

- unfortunately 죄송하지만
- change an appointment 약속을 변경하다
- reschedule a meeting appointment 회의 약속을 다시 잡다
- make it earlier 약속을 앞당기다
- make it later 약속을 늦추다
- postpone 연기하다, 늦추다
- be able to ~할 수 있다
- something has come up (예상치 못한) 일이 생기다

Warm up Dialogue

일정 변경 요청하기	응답하기
• I'm afraid I need to change my appointment.	• What day would be good for you?
• Something has come up, and I won't be able to make it.	• All right. Can we reschedule it to next week?
• I'm afraid I need to reschedule our appointment.	• How about Next Monday at 10 a.m. or 2 p.m.?

Key Expressions

- 10월 20일 미팅 건으로 전화드렸습니다.
  I'm calling about our meeting on October 20th.
- 죄송하지만 약속을 변경했으면 합니다.
  I'm afraid I need to reschedule our appointment.
  Unfortunately, I have to change our appointment.
- 죄송하지만 약속을 지키지 못할 것 같습니다.
  I'm afraid I won't be able to make it.
- 중요한 일이 생겨서 약속을 지키지 못할 것 같습니다.
  Something important has come up, and I won't be able to make it.
- 죄송하지만 회의 시간을 다시 잡아야 할 것 같습니다.
  I'm afraid we need to reschedule our meeting.
- 다음 주로 변경할 수 있을까요?
  Can we change it to next week?
  Can we make it to next week?
- 다른 시간으로 미룰 수 있을까요?
  Can we postpone it to another time?
- 다른 시간(날짜, 장소)으로 변경할 수 있을까요?
  Could we reschedule the meeting to another time / day / place?

Conversation Rescheduling a meeting

A Hello, this is Helen Oh, SNH Company speaking.
B This is Paul Kim from ABC Company calling.

A Hello, Mr. Kim.
B Hello, Ms. Oh. I apologize but I'm afraid we will need to reschedule our meeting for next Thursday. Something important has come up, and I won't be able to make it. Can we reschedule it to some other day?

A Sure, no problem. I'm available next Wednesday at 11 a.m. or at 3 p.m.
B Okay then shall we say next Wednesday at 11 a.m.?

A Sounds good, Mr. Kim.
B Thank you for being so flexible. I will see you on Wednesday.

Conversation Postponing a meeting

A Sun Industries, Chris Lee speaking.

B This is Paul Kim from ABC Company. I'm very sorry but I have a meeting to attend unexpectedly and will need to postpone our appointment that's scheduled for Friday morning.

A All right. When would you like to meet? I'm free next Tuesday.

B That works. What time shall we meet?

A Can we do it later, say at 2 p.m. or 3 p.m.?

B Yes, 3 p.m. would work for me.

A Good. I'll see you on December 7th at 3 p.m., Mr. Kim.

주요표현 연습(Pattern Drill)

1. 죄송하지만 약속을 변경했으면 합니다.

   ______________, I have to ______________ our appointment.

2. 다음 주로 변경할 수 있을까요?

   Can we ______________ it to next ______________?

3. 일이 생겨서 약속을 지키지 못할 것 같습니다.

   ______________ has come up, and I won't be ______________ to make it.

4. 다른 시간(날짜, 장소)으로 변경할 수 있을까요?

   Could we ______________ the meeting to ______________ time / day / place?

5. 죄송하지만 회의 시간을 다시 잡아야 할 것 같습니다.

   I'm ______________ we need to ______________ our meeting.

Unit 4

Cancelling a Meeting

Words and Phrases

- cancel an appointment 약속을 취소하다
- keep an appointment 약속을 지키다
- miss an appointment 약속을 지키지 못하다
- urgent 긴급한
- business trip 출장
- family emergency 가족에게 생긴 급한 일
- personal emergency 개인적으로 급한 일
- unexpected 예상치 못한
- unexpectedly 뜻밖에
- attend a meeting 회의에 참석하다
- take care of 돌보다
- sudden 갑작스런
- problem 문제
- flight 비행기
- delay 연기되다, 연기
- stick (교통체증으로) 꼼짝 못하다 (stick-stuck-stuck)
- traffic jam 교통체증
- break down 고장나다
- freeway 고속도로 (cf. highway 간선도로)
- settle down / clear up 해결되다

Warm up Dialogue

일정 취소 요청하기	응답하기
• I'm afraid I have to cancel our appointment. Can we reschedule it?	• Sure. Let me know when you're available.
• I have to go on a business trip unexpectedly. Can I postpone it to another time?	• No problem. When would be convenient for you?
• I'm terribly sorry, but I have to cancel our appointment tomorrow. I have a family emergency.	• I'm sorry to hear that. Just give me a call when your schedule clears up.

Key Expressions

- 죄송하지만 약속을 취소해야 할 것 같습니다. 긴급한 일이 생겼습니다.
  I'm afraid I have to cancel our appointment. Something urgent has come up.
- 갑작스럽게 출장을 가야 합니다.
  I have to go on a business trip unexpectedly.
- 가족에게(개인적으로) 급한 일이 생겨 약속을 지키지 못해 대단히 죄송합니다.
  I'm terribly sorry I missed our appointment. I have a family(personal) emergency.
- 정말 죄송합니다. 그리고 다른 시간을 잡았으면 합니다.
  I'm really sorry about this and I'd like to arrange another time.
- 예상치 못한 회의에 참석해야 합니다.
  I have to attend an unexpected meeting.
- 회사에 갑작스럽게 생긴 문제를 해결해야 합니다.
  I have to take care of a sudden problem in the company.
- 비행기가 3시간이나 연착되었습니다.
  My flight was delayed by three hours.
- 2시간 동안 교통체증에 걸렸습니다.
  I was stuck in a traffic jam for two hours.
- 차가 고속도로에서 고장 났습니다.
  My car broke down on the freeway.
- 유감이군요. 일정이 정리되시면 전화 부탁드립니다.
  I'm sorry to hear that. Just give me a call when your schedule clears up.

Conversation Cancelling a meeting

A Good morning, Paul Kim speaking.
B Good morning, Mr. Kim. This is Larry Smith from P&B Associations.

A Oh, yes. How are you doing?
B Fine, thank you. I'm calling to inform you that I have to go on a long business trip unexpectedly and will have to cancel our appointment tomorrow.

A Oh, I'm sorry to hear that.

B I apologize for the inconvenience. Let's schedule a meeting at another time once I'm back from the business trip.

A Oh, I understand. Just give me a call when your schedule clears up.

B I certainly will. Good bye.

주요표현 연습(Pattern Drill)

1. 죄송하지만 약속을 취소해야 할 것 같습니다.

   I'm afraid I have to ______________ our ______________________________.

2. 긴급한 일이 생겼습니다.

   Something __________________________ has ______________ up.

3. 갑작스럽게 출장을 가야 합니다.

   I have to __________ __________ a business trip unexpectedly.

4. 가족에게 급한 일이 생겼습니다.

   I have a ______________ ______________________________.

5. 출장에서 돌아오는 대로 다른 시간에 미팅을 잡도록 하죠.

   Let's ______________ a meeting at another time once I'm ______________ from the business ______________.

Unit 5

Scheduling a Meeting

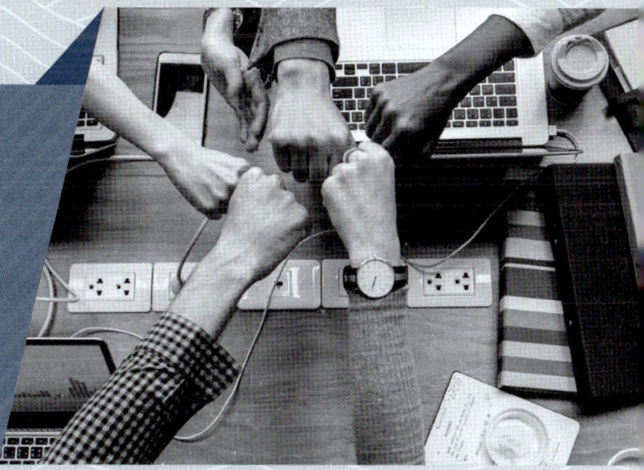

Words and Phrases

- fix a meeting 회의 날짜를 정하다
- before the end of the month 이 달 말 전에
- excellent idea 좋은 생각
- attend 참석하다
- general manager 부장
- at least 적어도
- sales & marketing manager 영업마케팅 매니저
- HR(Human Resources) 인사부서
- get in touch with ~와 연락하다
- participant 참가자
- get back 다시 알려주다

Warm up Dialogue

회의 일정 요청하기	해결하기
• Can we fix a meeting?	• When would be a good time?
• Who would you like to attend?	• Well, I'd like our general manager to attend.
• How much time do we need for the meeting?	• I think we need at least two hours.

Key Expressions

- 프로젝트를 논의할 회의를 잡았으면 합니다.
  I'd like to schedule a meeting to discuss the project.
- 회의 일정을 잡을 수 있을까요?
  Can we fix a meeting?
- 이 달 말 전에 만났으면 합니다.
  I'd like to see you before the end of the month.
- 정말 좋은 생각입니다.
  I think that would be an excellent idea.
- 누가 참석했으면 하십니까?
  Who would you like to attend?
- 부장이 참석했으면 합니다.
  Well, I'd like our general manager to attend.
- 회의시간은 얼마나 필요합니까?
  How much time do we need for the meeting?
- 2시간 정도는 잡아야 할 것 같습니다.
  I think we need at least two hours.
- 언제가 좋을까요?
  When would be a good time?
- 제가 영업마케팅 매니저에게 연락해서 편한 시간을 알아본 후 전화드리겠습니다.
  Let me get in touch with our sales & marketing manager to find a convenient time for everyone. Then I'll get back to you.
- 진행 상황을 알려주세요.
  Keep me posted.

Conversation Scheduling a meeting

A Hello, James.
B Hello, Nancy. I'd like to schedule a meeting to talk about our new project.

A I think that's a great idea. Who do you think should attend this meeting?
B Well, I'd like our HR director and head of our Sales & Marketing Department to attend.

A How much time do we need for the meeting?
B I think we will need at least two hours.

A Okay, let me first get in touch with them regarding the scheduling and I'll get back to you once we have a meeting scheduled.
B Sounds good. Keep me posted. Bye.

A Good bye.

주요표현 연습(Pattern Drill)

1. 회의 날짜를 정할까요?

_______________ we _______________ a meeting?

이 달 말 전에 만났으면 합니다.

I'd like to _______________ you _______________ the end of the month.

2. 누가 참석했으면 하십니까?

_______________ do you think should _______________ this meeting?

영업부장이 참석했으면 합니다.

I'd _______________ our _______________ manager to attend.

3. 회의시간은 얼마나 필요합니까?

How _______________ time do we _______________ for the meeting?

2시간 정도는 잡아야 할 것 같습니다.

I think we will need at _______________ two _______________.

4. 제가 영업마케팅 매니저에게 연락해 보겠습니다.

_______________ me get in _______________ with our Sales & Marketing manager.

그리고 나서 연락드리겠습니다.

Then I'll ___________ _______________ to you.

5. 정말 좋은 생각입니다.

I think that _______________ be an excellent _______________.

언제가 좋을까요?

_______________ would be a good _______________?

Unit 6 On-line Meeting

Words and Phrases

- create a new account 새 계정을 만들다
- set up a Zoom meeting 줌 미팅 일정을 잡다
- video conference call 화상회의
- sign up 회원 가입하다, 회원 등록하다
- sign in / log in 로그인하다
- download 다운로드하다
- join a meeting 회의에 참석하다
- host 회의 주최자
- participants 회의 참가자
- mute / unmute 음소거 / 음소거 해제
- start video / stop video 비디오 켜짐 / 비디오 꺼짐
- meeting link 회의주소 링크
- meeting ID / PW 회의 아이디 / 암호
- share screen 화면공유
- chat 채팅하다

Warm up Dialogue

줌 화상회의 일정 잡기	응답하기
• I'm calling to set up a Zoom meeting. When is the most appropriate time for you? • Would you be available for a Zoom meeting on Monday to discuss our new product?	• Let me check my schedule. How about this Monday morning or Wednesday afternoon? • Certainly. I look forward to receiving the Zoom link for our Monday meeting. Thanks.

Key Expressions

- 저희 신제품에 대한 논의를 위하여 월요일 오전 11시에 줌 미팅이 가능하신가요?
  Would you be available for a Zoom meeting on Monday at 11 a.m. to discuss our new product?
- 신입사원 교육에 대한 줌 미팅을 잡고 싶습니다.
  I would like to set up a Zoom meeting for you about our training new employees.
- 하루나 이틀 안에 줌 미팅 스케줄을 잡는 게 가능하신가요?
  Would it be possible for you to schedule a Zoom meeting in a day or two?
- Mr. Paul Kim과 전화 회의를 하고 싶습니다.
  I'd like to set up a conference call with Mr. Paul Kim.
- 미팅 가능한 날짜를 알려주시겠어요?
  Can you please let me know which dates would be possible?
- 시간이 안 되시면, 가장 좋은 날짜를 알려주시길 바랍니다.
  If the date doesn't work for you, please feel free to propose the best time for you.

Conversation On-line meeting

A Good morning, Paul Kim speaking.

B Good morning, Mr. Kim. This is Sandra Choi, Gina Kim's assistant, from SNH company. I'm calling to confirm Friday's Zoom meeting.

A Yes, I received an email from you with the Zoom meeting invite.

B Are you still available at 10:00 in the morning?

A Yes, 10 a.m. is fine.

B Great, please click on the Zoom link 5-10 minutes before the scheduled Zoom meeting so that the meeting can start on time.

A Yes, I will do that.

B Great. See you on Friday, Mr. Kim.

A Thanks for calling. See you then.

회의제목: 월간 그룹 미팅

회의 개최일시

회의 장소:
줌 회의이므로 링크주소

회의 초대문구
(Jane Hoya가 당신을 회의에 초대합니다)

회의 링크주소

회의 입장 ID

***패스워드 없는 경우:**
초청받은 누구나 자유롭게 회의참석 가능

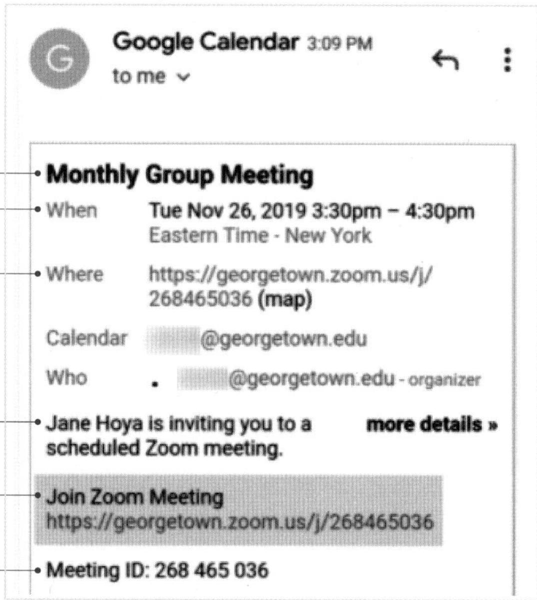

Google Calendar 3:09 PM
to me

Monthly Group Meeting
When Tue Nov 26, 2019 3:30pm – 4:30pm
Eastern Time - New York
Where https://georgetown.zoom.us/j/268465036 **(map)**
Calendar @georgetown.edu
Who • @georgetown.edu - organizer
Jane Hoya is inviting you to a scheduled Zoom meeting. **more details »**
Join Zoom Meeting
https://georgetown.zoom.us/j/268465036
Meeting ID: 268 465 036

제목: 회의 초대

회의 초대문구
(Marissa Perino가 당신을 회의에 초대합니다)

회의 주제

회의 개최 일시

회의 링크주소

회의 입장 ID

패스워드:
PW를 통해 회의에 들어오는 사람을 제한함

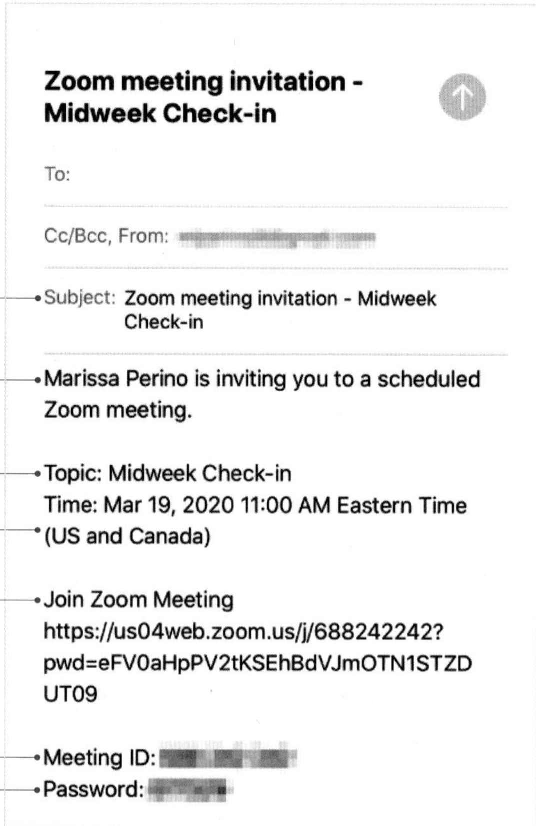

Zoom meeting invitation - Midweek Check-in
To:
Cc/Bcc, From:
Subject: Zoom meeting invitation - Midweek Check-in
Marissa Perino is inviting you to a scheduled Zoom meeting.
Topic: Midweek Check-in
Time: Mar 19, 2020 11:00 AM Eastern Time (US and Canada)
Join Zoom Meeting
https://us04web.zoom.us/j/688242242?pwd=eFV0aHpPV2tKSEhBdVJmOTN1STZDUT09
Meeting ID:
Password:

On-line Meeting Etiquette

1. 약속보다 일찍 입장한다
   Don't' be late. Open the meeting room early.
2. 화상회의 툴 사용법을 미리 익힌다
   Practice with the technology.
3. 회의 중에 이동하지 않는다
   Sit still.
4. 소리의 울림이 없도록 헤드셋 또는 마이크를 이용한다
   Use the headset(microphone) not to make howling.
5. 카메라 밖으로 숨지 않는다
   Turn on the camera.
6. 회의에 집중한다
   Focus on the agenda and don't multitask.
7. 내가 말하지 않을 때는 음소거를 한다
   Keep yourself on mute unless you're speaking.
8. 말하기 전에 이름을 밝혀라
   Say your name before you speak.
9. 단순한 배경을 택한다
   Have a clean-work-appropriate background.
10. 핸드폰을 무음으로 한다
    You should put your cell phone on mute.

*출처: Video meeting etiquette: 7 tips to ensure a great attendee experience

Grammar Point

❶ 장소 전치사(Prepositions of Place)

'on' with street – 거리 이름 앞에 쓴다.

Ex. The post office is on Third Avenue.

'at' with address – 주소 앞에 쓴다.

Ex. We work at 14 Maple Street.

'in' with city, state, country, continent – 도시, 주, 나라, 대륙 이름 앞에 쓴다.

Ex. My family lives in Mexico City.

Prepositions of Place(장소 전치사)

in		on		at	
room	in the living room	street	on Main Street	buildings	at the store
	in the office		on York Street		at the bank
city	in Boston	floor	on the first floor		at work
state	in California		on the fifth floor		at school
country	in Canada	house	on the porch		at home
house	in the basement		on the deck	address	at 12 North Avenue
	in the yard				
	in the garage				

Practicing on Your Own

Ⓐ Refer to the chart in the above and complete each sentence with *in, on,* or *at.* (위 표를 보고 전치사 in, on, at을 넣어 문장을 완성하세요)

1. His office is __________ the seventh floor.

2. Susan is __________ work now.

3. The office building is __________ Broad Street.

4. Peter isn't __________ his office now. He's __________ the bank.

Unit 6 On-line Meeting

5. After work, I sit __________ the deck and relax.

6. Some employees of our company work __________ home.

7. There are branch offices __________ Taiwan and Japan.

8. He works __________ Seoul.

B **Complete the following sentences using the prepositions of time: *for* or *until*.** (시간 전치사 for 또는 until를 넣어 문장을 완성하세요)

1. I'll be away __________ five days.

2. I'll be away __________ the end of this month.

3. You must finish the report __________ this weekend.

4. I'm going on a business trip __________ two weeks.

Language Check

Here is Gina Kim's diary for the week. (이번주 Gina Kim의 일정표)

Monday	Tuesday	Wednesday	Thursday	Friday
12.30	10.00	10.00	8.00	
lunch with	sales	factory	flight to Paris	
Joe	meeting	visit		

Complete Gina Kim's description of her appointments with the correct prepositions from the list. In three of spaces no preposition is necessary. (박스에서 알맞은 전치사를 골라 Gina Kim의 약속을 완성하세요. 단, 이 중 세 개는 전치사가 필요 없습니다)

on	in	at	to	with	for

1. ________ today I'm having lunch ________ Joe.
2. ________ tomorrow morning ________ ten I'm going ________ a sales meeting.
3. I'm visiting ________ the factory ________ Wednesday ________ the morning.
4. I'm flying ________ Paris ______ the training course ______ Friday ____ 8 a.m.

Work in pairs

First, study the example dialog. Then make up similar dialogs about the other days using the calendar in pairs. (먼저 예시 대화를 살펴보세요. 달력을 보고 다른 날짜를 이용하여 비슷한 대화를 만드세요)

Example dialogue (Today is January 21st.)

A So, when can we get together?
B Let me see… How about the day after tomorrow?

A That's the 23rd, right?
B That's right.

a. this Friday

b. a week from tomorrow

c. next Monday

d. next Sunday

e. a week from Tuesday

JANUARY						
SUN	MON	TUES	WED	THURS	FRI	SAT
		1	2	3	4	5
6	7	8	9	10	11	12
13	14	15	16	17	18	19
20	21	22	23	24	25	26
27	28	29	30	31		

Daily Office English Conversation
사무영어회화

Chapter 05

Business Trip

01
Making and Confirming Flight Reservations

•

02
Checking in for a Flight

•

03
Making Hotel Reservations

•

04
Making Restaurant Reservations

•

05
Renting a Car

•

06
Sightseeing & Korean Culture

Unit 1 Making and Confirming Flight Reservations

Words and Phrases

- reserve / book / make a reservation 예약하다
- confirm a reservation 예약을 확인하다
- flight / plane 비행기
- flight number 항공편 번호
- reservation number 예약 번호
- confirmation number 예약 확인번호
- seat 좌석
- economy class / coach class 일반석
- business class 비즈니스석
- first class 일등석
- ticket 항공권
- one-way ticket 편도 항공권
- round-trip ticket 왕복 항공권
- return ticket 돌아오는 비행기 항공권
- direct flight / nonstop flight 직항 항공편
- departure time 출발 시간
- arrival time 도착 시간
- local time 현지 시간
- connecting flight 연결 항공편
- destination 목적지
- final destination 최종 목적지
- leave 출발하다
- arrive 도착하다

Warm up Dialogue

항공편 예약하기	응답하기
• I'd like to reserve a seat for New York.	• Yes, sir. When would you like to leave?
• When does the flight arrive in New York?	• The flight arrives at 3:30 p.m.
• Is this nonstop flight?	• No. The flight makes one stop in Anchorage.
• I'd like to confirm a reservation for flight on May 1st from Inchon to Paris.	• May I have your name and confirmation number?

Key Expressions

- 9월 1일 샌프란시스코행 좌석을 예약하고 싶습니다.
  I'd like to make a reservation to San Francisco on September 1st.
- 다음 주 토요일 뉴욕행 좌석을 예약하려고 합니다.
  I'd like to book a seat for New York for next Saturday.
- 도쿄행 왕복 티켓 부탁합니다.
  I'd like a round trip ticket to Tokyo.
- 인천에서 오전 10시30분에 출발하는 비행기가 있습니다.
  We have a flight leaving Inchon at 10:30 a.m.
- 비행기는 언제 출발하나요?
  What time does the flight leave?
- 비행기는 오전 10시에 출발합니다.
  The flight leaves at 10 a.m.
- 비행기가 언제 뉴욕에 도착하나요?
  When does the flight arrive in New York?
- 비행기는 오후 6시에 도착합니다.
  The flight arrives at 6 p.m.
- 비행기는 직항입니다.
  The flight is direct.
  The flight is nonstop.
- 그 비행기는 도쿄에서 한 번 십니다.
  The flight makes one stop in Tokyo.
- 어떤 등급의 좌석을 원하십니까?
  What class of seat do you want?

- 일반석 / 비즈니스석 / 일등석 부탁드립니다.
  Economy class / business class / first class, please.
- 얼마입니까?
  How much will that cost?
- 왕복 2,300불입니다.
  It costs $2,300 round trip.
- 예약을 확인하고 싶어서 전화했습니다.
  I'm calling to confirm my reservation.
- 5월 10일 인천에서 파리로 가는 비행기 예약을 확인하고 싶습니다.
  I'd like to confirm a reservation for flight on May 10th from Inchon to Paris.
- 성함과 예약 확인번호를 알려주시겠습니까?
  May I have your name and confirmation number?

Conversation Booking a flight

A Korean Airlines, may I help you?
B I'd like to book a round trip ticket to Paris.

A Yes, sir. When would you like to leave?
B This Sunday.

A All right. We have a flight leaving at 10 a.m. this Sunday.
B Great.

A Would you like coach or business class seating?
B Business class, please. How much will that cost?

A It comes up to $6,000 for the round trip flight. Shall I go ahead and reserve it?
B Yes, please. Thanks.

주요표현 연습(Pattern Drill)

1. 뉴욕행 비행기를 예약하고 싶습니다.

I'd like to ____________ a seat for New York.

인천에서 오전 10시30분에 출발하는 비행기가 있습니다.

We have a flight ____________ Inchon ____________ 10:30 a.m.

2. 비행기가 언제 출발하나요?

What ____________ does the ____________ leave?

비행기는 오전 11시에 출발합니다.

The flight ____________________ ________ 11 a.m.

3. 어떤 등급의 좌석을 원하십니까?

What ______________ of seat do you ____________?

일반석을 부탁드립니다.

______________________ class, please.

4. 얼마입니까?

How _______________ will that _________________?

왕복 6,000불입니다.

It ____________ up to $6,000 for the ____________ trip flight.

5. 비행기가 뉴욕에 언제 도착하나요?

____________ does the flight ____________ in New York?

비행기는 오후 5시에 도착합니다.

The flight ____________ ________ 5 p.m.

Unit 2 Checking in for a Flight

Words and Phrases

- check-in 탑승 수속, 체크인
- carry-on bag 기내 휴대용 가방
- board 탑승하다
- boarding pass 탑승권
- boarding time 탑승 시각
- gate 탑승구
- luggage / baggage 수하물, 짐
- baggage claim 수하물 찾는 곳
- security check 보안 검사
- seat preference 좌석 선호
- window seat 창가 좌석
- aisle seat 통로 쪽 좌석
- customs declaration form 세관 신고서
- declare 신고하다
- prohibited items 금지품목
- purpose of visit 방문목적

Warm up Dialogue

탑승 수속하기	응답하기
• How many bags are you checking in?	• I'd like to check two bags.
• Would you prefer a window or an aisle seat?	• I'd like an aisle seat.
• What's the purpose of your visit?	• I'm going on a business trip.

Key Expressions

- 몇 개의 가방을 부치십니까?
  How many bags are you checking in?
- 가방 2개를 부치고 싶습니다.
  I'd like to check two bags.
  I have two bags to check in.
- 창가와 통로 쪽 어느 쪽 좌석을 원하십니까?
  Would you prefer a window or an aisle seat?
- 창가 쪽 좌석을 원합니다.
  I'd like a window seat.
- 좋아하는 좌석이 있으십니까?
  Do you have a seat preference?
- 7C 좌석을 드리겠습니다.
  I'll give you seat 7C.
- 탑승권과 여권 부탁드립니다.
  Your boarding pass and passport, please.
- 여기 탑승권입니다.
  Here's your boarding pass
- 30분 후에 7A 탑승구에서 탑승하시면 됩니다.
  You can board at gate 7A after 30 minutes.
- 방문 목적이 무엇입니까?
  What's the purpose of your visit?
- 출장 갑니다.
  I'm going on a business trip.
- 얼마 동안 머무르십니까?
  How long are you staying?
  How long will you be staying?
- (세관) 신고하실 게 있으십니까?
  Do you have anything to declare?
- (세관) 신고할 게 없습니다.
  I have nothing to declare.
- 안전한 여행 되세요.
  Have a safe trip.

Conversation Checking in for a flight

A May I have your ticket, please?
B Here you go.

A Are you going to Chicago?
B Yes, that's right.

A How many bags are you checking in?
B Just two.

A Would you prefer a window seat or an aisle seat?
B Window seat, please.

A Okay, I can give you seat 24A. Here's your boarding pass.
B Thank you.

A Thank you very much.

주요표현 연습(Pattern Drill)

1. 방문 목적이 무엇입니까?

What's the ________________ of your ________________?

출장 갑니다.

I'm ________________ on a business ________________.

2. 체크인할 가방이 몇 개 인가요?

How ________________ bags are you ____________ __________?

가방 2개를 부치고 싶습니다.

I have ________________ bags to ________________ in.

3. 창가와 통로 쪽 어느 쪽 좌석을 원하십니까?

Would you __________________ a window or an __________________ seat?

창가 쪽 좌석을 원합니다.

I'd like a __________________ seat.

4. 탑승권과 여권 부탁드립니다.

Your __________________ pass and __________________, please.

여기 탑승권입니다.

____________ __________ your boarding pass.

5. (세관) 신고하실 것이 있습니까?

Do you have __________________ to __________________?

신고할 것이 없습니다.

I have __________________ to __________________.

Unit 3

Making Hotel Reservations

Words and Phrases

- check in 입실 수속하다, 체크인하다
- check out 퇴실 수속하다, 체크아웃하다
- front desk (호텔) 안내 데스크, 프런트 데스크
- lobby 로비
- room rate 객실 요금
- vacancy 빈방
- single room 1인실(싱글 침대가 하나인 객실)
- double room 2인실(더블 침대가 하나인 객실)
- twin room 트윈 룸(싱글 침대가 2개인 객실)
- suite room 스위트 룸(거실이 있는 객실)
- a room with an ocean view 바다가 보이는 방
- room service 룸서비스(음식이나 음료를 객실로 가져다 주는 서비스)
- laundry service 세탁물 서비스
- wake-up call / morning call 전화로 손님을 깨워주는 서비스
- complimentary breakfast 무료 조식
- business center 투숙객의 사무를 위해 인터넷, 복사, 팩스 등 비즈니스 업무가 가능한 곳
- concierge service 투숙객의 편의를 위해 다양한 정보나 불편사항을 도와주는 서비스
- mini bar 호텔 객실의 냉장고에 유료로 음료수, 주류, 스낵 등을 갖추어 놓은 곳
- personal safe 개인 금고
- cancellation fee 취소 수수료
- fitness center 운동 시설
- airport shuttle 공항 셔틀 버스
- amenities (호텔에 갖춰져 있는)편의 시설, 편의 용품

Warm up Dialogue

호텔 예약하기	응답하기
• I'd like to book a single room, please.	• When do you need it , sir?
• I would like a room with an ocean view.	• I'll check if it's available now.
• How much do you charge per night?	• That'll be $150 per night.

Key Expressions

- 9월 1일부터 3일까지 더블 룸 하나를 예약하고 싶습니다.
  I'd like to book a double room from September 1st to 3rd.
- 얼마나 머무실 겁니까?
  How long would you like to stay?
- 싱글 룸과 더블 룸 중 어느 것을 원하십니까?
  Would you like a single or double room?
- 바다가 보이는 방을 원합니다.
  I'd like a room with an ocean view.
- 흡연 룸과 금연 룸 중 어느 것을 원하십니까?
  Would you prefer smoking or nonsmoking room?
- 죄송합니다만 주말에는 모두 예약이 되었습니다.
  I'm sorry, but we're all booked for the weekend.
- 오늘 묵을 방이 있습니까?
  Do you have any vacancies today?
- 성함과 휴대폰 번호를 여쭤봐도 될까요?
  May I ask your name and mobile phone number, please?
- 어떻게 결제하시겠습니까?
  How will you be paying?
- 신용카드로 계산할 수 있습니까?
  Can I pay with my credit card?
- 객실 요금이 얼마입니까?
  What's the rate for the room?
  How much do you charge per night?
- 어느 분으로 예약되어 있나요?
  What name is it under?
- 이번 주 금요일로 예약한 방을 취소하고 싶습니다.
  I'd like to cancel the room reserved for this Friday.
  I'd like to cancel my reservation for this Friday.

Conversation Making a hotel reservation

A Marriott Hotel, may I help you?
B Hello. I'd like to book a single room, please.

A When do you need it, ma'am?
B For the nights of August 1st to 3rd.

A Certainly, ma'am. Would you like a room with an ocean view?
B Yes, please.

A May I ask for your name, please?
B Gina Kim. How much is it per night?

A It's $150 per night.

주요표현 연습(Pattern Drill)

1. 싱글 룸을 예약하고 싶습니다.

   I'd like to __________ a __________ room, please.

2. 얼마나 머무실 겁니까?

   How __________ would you like to __________?

3. 바다가 보이는 방을 원합니다.

   I'd __________ a room with an __________ view.

4. 죄송합니다만 주말에는 모두 예약이 되었습니다.

   I'm sorry, but we're __________ __________ for the __________.

5. 일박 가격이 얼마입니까?

   How __________ is it __________ night?

Unit 4

Making Restaurant Reservations

Words and Phrases

- fully booked / completely booked 예약이 꽉 찬
- put down~ (리스트에) 이름을 올리다
- waitlist 대기자 명단
- reserve a table for four 4명 자리를 예약하다
- make a reservation for two 2명 자리를 예약하다
- make a note 기재하다
- reservation book 예약 장부
- recommend 추천하다
- party 일행
- regular customer 단골손님
- guarantee 보증하다
- be ready to order ~를 주문할 준비가 되다
- have a look at the menu 메뉴를 훑어보다
- today's special dish 오늘의 특별 요리
- add 추가하다
- quiet table 조용한 테이블

Warm up Dialogue

식당 예약하기	해결하기
• I'd like to reserve a table for two on Saturday night.	• What time will it be?
• Could I reserve a table for Friday evening?	• I'm sorry, but we are fully booked.
• I'd like to book a table for this evening.	• How many people are there in your party?

Key Expressions

- 토요일 저녁 7시에 두 사람의 자리를 예약하고 싶습니다.
  I'd like to reserve a table for two on Saturday night at 7 p.m.
  I'd like to make a reservation for two on Saturday night at 7 p.m.
- 조용한 테이블로 예약할 수 있을까요?
  Could we have a quiet table, please?
  Can I make a reservation for a quiet table?
- 몇 시로 예약하시겠습니까?
  What time would you like the reservation?
- 일행이 몇 분인가요?
  How many people are there in your party?
- 죄송하지만, 예약이 꽉 찼습니다.
  I'm sorry, but we are fully booked.
  I'm sorry, but we are completely booked.
- 대기자 명단에 저를 올려주시겠어요?
  Can you please put me down on the waitlist?
- 어느 분으로 예약해 드릴까요?
  Under what name, please?
  May I have your name, please?
- 일행을 기다리고 있는 중입니다.
  We are expecting someone else.
- 죄송하지만, 예약을 취소해야 할 것 같습니다.
  I'm afraid I need to cancel my reservation.

Conversation Making a restaurant reservation

A Good morning. O'la Restaurant, may I help you?
B I'd like to reserve a table for three this evening.

A Let me check my reservation book. I'm sorry, but we are fully booked for the night.
B I see. Can you please put me down on the waitlist?

A Certainly. May I have your name, please?
B My name is Jessica Brown and the number is 010-5333-7777.

A Great. I'll call you by 5 o'clock in the afternoon if we have any availabilities. Good bye.
B Thank you. Good bye.

주요표현 연습(Pattern Drill)

1. 오늘 저녁 두 명 자리를 예약하고 싶습니다.

   I'd like to ______________ a table ______________ two this ______________.

2. 몇 시로 예약하시겠습니까?

   ______________ time would you like the ______________?

3. 일행이 몇 분인가요?

   How ______________ people are there in your ______________?

4. 죄송하지만 예약이 꽉 찼습니다.

   I'm sorry, but we are ______________ ______________.

5. 대기자 명단에 저를 올려주시겠어요?

   Can you please ______________ me down on the ______________?

Unit 5

Renting a Car

Words and Phrases

- rent 빌리다
- rent-a-car company 렌터카 회사
- rent-a-car service 자동차 임대 서비스
- compact car 소형차
- mid-size car / standard-size car 중형차
- full-size car 대형차
- SUV(Sport Utility Vehicle) 스포츠 유틸리티 차량
- rental rate 렌탈 요금
- date of return 반납일
- insurance 보험
- coverage 보험 적용 범위
- comprehensive coverage 종합 보험
- deposit 보증금
- agreement 동의서
- driver's license 운전 면허증
- highway / freeway / expressway 고속도로
- crosswalk 횡단보도
- detour 우회도로
- intersection 교차로

Warm up Dialogue

차 렌트하기	응답하기
• I'd like to rent a car. • I'd like a compact car, please. • How long would you like to rent it for? • How much is the rental rate?	• What size car would you like? • Let me see what we' ve got left. • I'll need it for a week. • It's $70 per day.

Key Expressions

- 차를 빌리고 싶습니다.
  I'd like to rent a car, please.
- 어떤 사이즈 차를 원하십니까?
  What size car would you like?
- 소형 차를 찾고 있습니다.
  I'm looking for a compact car.
- 남아있는 차가 어떤 게 있는지 보겠습니다.
  Let me see what we've got left.
- 얼마 동안 빌리실 건가요?
  How long would you like to rent it for?
- 일주일 동안 필요합니다.
  I'll need it for a week.
- 렌탈 요금은 얼마입니까?
  How much is the rental rate?
- 일일 요금이 얼마입니까?
  What's the daily rate?
- 주간 요금이 얼마입니까?
  What's the weekly rate?
- 하루에 50달러입니다.
  It's $50 per day.
- 보험이 포함됩니까?
  Does that include insurance?

Conversation Renting a car

A Good morning, may I help you?
B I'd like to rent a car, please.

A What size car would you like?
B I'm looking for a mid-size car, please.

A Sure. We currently have a Hyundai Genesis 80.
B I see. How much is the rental rate for that vehicle?

A It's $100 per day, including the insurance. How long would you like to rent it for?
B I'll need it for a week.

A (few minutes later) Okay, here is your rental agreement. I will need your credit card and your driver's license to finalize the reservation.
B Sure. Here's my Visa card and my driver's license.

A (few minutes later) You're all set. Here are the keys. Thank you.

주요표현 연습(Pattern Drill)

1. 차를 빌리고 싶습니다.

   I'd ______________ to ______________ a car, please.

   어떤 사이즈 차를 원하십니까?

   ______________ size __________ would you like?

2. 소형 차를 찾고 있습니다.

   I'm ______________ for a ______________ car.

   남아있는 차가 어떤 게 있는지 보겠습니다.

   Let me ______________ what we've ______________ left.

3. 얼마 동안 빌리실 건가요?

   How ______________ would you like to ______________ it for?

   일주일입니다.

   I'll ______________ it for a ______________.

4. 그 차량에 대한 렌탈 요금이 얼마입니까?

   ______________ much is the rental rate for that ______________?

   보험을 포함하여 하루에 50달러입니다.

   It's $50 ______________ day, including the ______________.

5. 여기 비자카드와 운전면허증 있습니다.

   ______________ __________ my Visa card and my driver's license.

   모두 처리되었습니다. 여기 열쇠입니다.

   You're all ______________. Here are the ______________

Unit 5 Renting a Car

Unit 6

Sightseeing & Korean Culture

Words and Phrases

- historical 역사적인
- historic site 유적지
- famous 유명한
- tourist information 관광 안내소
- tourist attraction 관광지
- tour guide 여행 가이드
- tour bus 관광 버스
- sights 명소
- national museum 국립 박물관
- national treasure 국보
- folk village 민속촌
- go sightseeing 관광하다
- admission fee 입장료
- souvenir 기념품
- traditional 전통적인
- Korean traditional liquor 한국 전통 주
- Korean dish 한국 음식
- traditional food 전통 음식
- side dish 반찬
- rice wine 막걸리
- full course Korean meal 한정식
- chopsticks 젓가락
- spoon 숟가락

Warm up Dialogue

한국 문화 소개하기	응답하기
• Are you interested in taking a sight-seeing of Gyeongju? • I'd like to try Korean traditional food. • Where can I find some Korean souvenir?	• Yes. I'd like to see the sights of Gyeongju. • Would you like to try bulgogi? • There are a lot of souvenirs in Insa-dong, Chongno.

Key Expressions

- 관광 안내소는 어디에 있습니까?
  Where is the tourist information?
- 민속촌을 관광하고 싶습니다.
  I'd like to take a tour of folk village.
- 유적지 관광을 안내해 드릴까요?
  Would you like me to show you around the historical site?
- 여기 머무는 동안 가보고 싶은 곳이 있으세요?
  Is there any place you want to visit while you're here?
- 서울에 있는 유적지를 보고 싶습니다.
  I'd like to see some historical sites in Seoul.
- 어떤 관광이 있습니까?
  What kinds of tours are there?
- 오전 관광으로 하겠습니다.
  I'll take the morning tour.
- 서울 야간 관광에 관심 있나요?
  Are you interested in taking a night tour of Seoul?
- 입장료는 얼마인가요?
  How much is the admission fee?
- 점심식사로 무엇을 드시겠습니까?
  What would you like to have for lunch?
- 저녁 먹으러 가실까요?
  Shall we go out for dinner?
- 유명한 한국 음식 뭐가 있나요?
  What is a well-known Korean dish?
- 근처에 점심 먹을 괜찮은 곳을 추천해 줄 수 있나요?
  Can you recommend a good place for lunch nearby?
- 불고기 한번 드셔보시겠어요?
  Would you like to try bulgogi?
- 오늘 밤 무슨 계획이라도 있으세요?
  Do you have any plans for tonight?
- 한국 음식은 좀 매워요.
  Korean food is a little spicy.
- 저녁 잘 먹었습니다.
  Dinner was delicious.
- 저녁식사에 초대해 주셔서 감사합니다.
  Thank you for inviting me out for dinner.

Conversation Sightseeing

A I'd like to visit historical sites in Seoul. Are there any sightseeing services available?

B Of course. There are city bus tours available. When would you like to go?

A Are there any tours available this afternoon?

B Yes. Do you want me to make a reservation for you?

A How much is it for the afternoon tour?

B It's $8 for adults.

A Great. Please go ahead and book the afternoon tour for me.

Conversation Introducing Korean food

A Do you have any plans for tonight?

B Nothing in particular.

A Then would you like to join us for dinner tonight?

B That would be wonderful. Thank you.

A Have you ever tried bulgogi and naengmyeon?

B No. Could you explain what they are?

A They are both famous Korean dishes - Bulgogi is made of thinly sliced, marinated beef and naengmyeon is cold noodle soup.

B They both sound amazing. I would love to try them!

주요표현 연습(Pattern Drill)

1. 서울에 있는 유적지를 보고 싶습니다.

   I'd like to ____________ historical sites ____________ Seoul.

   시티버스 투어가 가능합니다. 언제 가기를 원하시나요?

   There are city bus tours ____________. When would you like to ____________?

2. 오후 투어가 얼마입니까?

   How ____________ is it ____________ the afternoon tour?

   성인 기준 8불입니다.

   ____________ is $8 ____________ adults.

3. 오늘 저녁식사 저희와 함께하시겠어요?

   Would you like to ____________ us for ____________tonight?

   좋습니다. 고맙습니다.

   ____________ would be wonderful. ____________ you.

4. 불고기와 냉면 드셔보신 적 있으세요?

   ____________ you ever ____________ bulgogi and naengmyeon?

   아뇨. 그것에 대해 설명해 주시겠어요?

   No. Could you ____________ what they are?

5. 저녁 잘 먹었습니다.

   Dinner was ____________________.

   저녁식사에 초대해 주셔서 감사합니다.

   Thank you for ____________________ me out for ______________.

Grammar Point

1 기수(Cardinal number)와 서수(Ordinal number)

- 영어로 숫자를 읽는 법은 기수와 서수 두 가지이다. 기수는 수를 세는 '기본수'이고 서수는 사물의 순서를 나타내거나 날짜를 읽을 때 사용된다.
- 미국식으로 표기할 때에는 월, 일, 연도의 순으로 표기하고, 영국식으로는 일, 월, 연도의 순서이고 콤마를 사용하지 않는다.

  미국식 표기: March 25th, 2022

  영국식 표기: 25th March 2022

[서수 표기법]

1st = first	11th = eleventh	21st = twenty-first
2nd = second	12th = twelfth	30th = thirtieth
3rd = third	13th = thirteenth	32nd = thirty-second
4th = fourth	14th = fourteenth	40th = fortieth
5th = fifth	15th = fifteenth	50th = fiftieth
6th = sixth	16th = sixteenth	60th = sixtieth
7th = seventh	17th = seventeenth	70th = seventieth
8th = eighth	18th = eighteenth	80th = eightieth
9th = ninth	19th = nineteenth	90th = ninetieth
10th= tenth	20th = twentieth	100th=hundredth

❷ Adverbs of frequency(빈도부사)

Use: Adverbs and expressions of frequency tell how often we do something and often used with the simple present tense. (빈도부사는 우리가 얼마나 자주 무엇을 하는지를 표현하고 현재 시제로 사용함)

Place adverbs of frequency after the verb *be.*

be동사	빈도부사	
Gina is	always usually often sometimes rarely never	on time.

Place adverbs of frequency before the *other verbs.*

	빈도부사	other verbs(일반동사)
Gina	always usually often sometimes rarely never	listen to music.

Practicing on Your Own

Ⓐ Complete the sentences. Choose the correct numbers. (Grammar Point 1을 참조하여 문장에 알맞은 기수와 서수를 고르세요)

1. My classroom is on the ______________ (two, second) floor.
2. My ______________ (one, first) class is at nine-thirty.
3. Sue is ______________ (twenty-three, twenty-third) years old.

4. The bookstore is on ____________ (Five, Fifth) Avenue.

5. ____________ (Three, Third) apples are green, and ____________ (six, sixth) are red.

6. November is the ____________ (eleven, eleventh) month of the year.

B **Complete the sentences. Use the correct form of the verbs and the adverbs of frequency in parentheses.** (괄호 안의 동사와 빈도부사를 이용하여 문장을 완성하세요)

1. Lulu ____________ (be, often) early. She ____________ (wait, usually) for other people.

2. Pete ____________ (be, often) late. He ____________ (get, rarely) to work on time.

3. Elenore ____________ (be, usually) on time. She ____________ (come, rarely) late.

4. Norma ____________ (be, always) early for meetings.

5. Carol is like her father. She ____________ (be, usually) late for everything.

Language Check

A **Match the questions on the left with the best response on the right.** (다음 대화를 연결하세요)

______ 1. What do you do?	• a. No, I'm from China.
______ 2. Do you like it here?	• b. For one month.
______ 3. Are you from Japan?	• c. I'm an engineer.
______ 4. How long have you been here?	• d. Yes, I have two kids.

_________ 5. Do you have any children?

_________ 6. How do you like this weather?

• e. I'm afraid it's too hot and humid for me.

• f. Yes, I like here very much.

Ⓑ **Complete each question to fit the answer provided.** (아래 주어진 답변에 맞는 질문을 완성하세요)

Ex. Q: What is your name?
A: My name is John Smith.

1. Q: What ______________________________?
   A: I'm an engineer. I work for Ace Computer.

2. Q: How ______________________________?
   A: My daughter is 15 and my boy is 11.

3. Q: How ______________________________?
   A: Very much! I love the weather here.

4. Q: How long ______________________________?
   A: I've been here for about six months.

Work in pairs

Situation. Ms. Gina Kim의 어시스턴트인 Sanda Choi가 상사의 홍콩 출장을 위해 해당 호텔에 직접 전화를 걸어 룸을 예약하는 상황

Receptionist: Hotel front desk **Choi:** Sandra Choi

R	Good morning, reservations. May I help you?
C	I'd like to reserve a room, please.
R	For when would you like the room?
C	For the nights of May 1st to the 5th.

↓ ↓

A: 예약 대기를 요청하는 경우

R I'm sorry we're fully booked on that date.

↓

C Can you put my name on the waitlist, then?

↓

R Sure. May I have your name, please?

↓

C Sandra Choi and my number is 010-222-3333.

↓

R I'll put your name on the waitlist.

↓

C Thank you.

B: 예약이 가능한 경우

R Yes, we have a double room for those dates.

↓

C I'd like to reserve a room under the name of Ms. Gina Kim.

↓

R May I have your credit card number to guarantee your reservation?

↓

C It's 1234-5678-9000. It expires in March 2023. How much is the rate?

↓

R It will cost $230 per night during week days, and $250 during week-ends. May I have your name?

↓

C Gina Kim.

↓

R We'll reserve a room from May 1st to the 5th under the name Ms. Gina Kim.

↓

C Thank you.

↓

R Thanks for calling.

Sample Expressions

예약 요청하기	응답하기
• I'd like to book a double room, please. • I'll be staying for two nights from Friday to Sunday. • How much do you charge per night? / What's the rate for the room?	• When is it for? / For what date? • Yes, we have a double room for those dates. • A double room starts from 230 dollars per night.

Chapter 06

Business Email

01
Email Format

•

02
Email Abbreviation

•

03
Key Expressions Used in Email

•

04
Sample Email Templates

Unit 1 Email Format

- 최근에 공식적인 상황을 제외하고는 비즈니스에서 가장 보편적으로 사용되는 영문서이다.
- 문서와 동일한 효력을 가진다.
- 비즈니스 레터에서 사용하는 형식적인 요소 등은 생략하고, 상황과 수신인에 따라 격식을 갖추어 사용한다.

[E-mail]

To:	수신인, 이메일 주소
Cc:	참조 수신인, 이메일 주소
Bcc:	숨은 참조(수신인 및 참조 수신인에게 보이지 않음)
From:	발송인, 이메일 주소
Date:	발송 날짜
Subject:	제목
Attachment:	첨부 파일
이메일 본문	

Ⓐ Basic Components

이메일은 기본적으로 To, From, Date, Subject, Body로 구성된다.

a. To (수신인)
이메일을 받는 이의 e-mail 주소를 기입한다.

b. From (발신인)

- 보내는 사람의 e-mail 주소를 쓰는 곳이다.
- 일반적으로 소프트웨어를 작동한 시점에서는 발신인의 e-mail 주소가 자동으로 기입되어 상대방에게 보여진다.

c. Date (발신 일자)

- 보통 문서의 첫머리에 발신한 일자와 시간이 나오므로 입력할 필요가 없는 경우가 대부분이다.

d. Subject (제목)

- 전체 내용을 간략히 요약하여 기입한다.
- 수신인의 입장에서는 제목만 보고 먼저 읽을 것을 결정하는 경우가 많으므로 신중하게 생각해서 작성한다.

e. Body (본문)

- 일반적으로 형식적인 인사말은 피하고 간단한 인사와 함께 바로 본론으로 들어간다.
- 전하고자 하는 내용도 결론부터 먼저 쓰고 이유나 과정을 다음에 쓴다.
- 문단 사이는 1행 띄어 읽기 쉽게 하고 e-mail 약어(abbreviation) 등은 일반적으로 널리 알려진 것이나 상대방이 확실히 이해할 수 있는 것만을 사용한다.

Ⓑ Additional Components

추가적인 요소로 Carbon Copy, Blind Carbon Copy, Attachment가 있다.

a. Carbon Copy(cc, 사본 송부처)

- 동일 내용의 e-mail을 수신인 이외의 관련된 사람이나 부서 사람에게 한 번에 보낼 수 있다.
- 여러 사람인 경우 comma(,)나 semicolon(;)으로 연결할 수 있다.

b. Blind Carbon Copy(bcc, 감추어진 사본 송부처)

- 수신인이나 사본 수신인이 모르게 제삼자에게 보내는 경우 사용한다.
- 제삼자의 e-mail 주소를 bcc(숨은 참조)칸에 쓴다.

c. Attachment(첨부)

- 본문의 내용과 관련된 자료를 함께 보내고자 할 때 해당 파일을 첨부한다.
- 긴 자료나 화상 데이터 등을 따로 첨부하는 경우, Attachment란에 그 내용을 명시하고 자료 첨부 기능의 명령을 실행시킨다.
- 첨부파일 제목은 파일 내용을 알 수 있도록 작성한다.
- 첨부파일은 적을수록 좋으며, 최대한 본문에 삽입한다. 첨부파일이 여러 개라면, 각 첨부파일에 어떤 내용이 있는지 적어준다.
- 워드, 파워포인트, 한글의 경우 PDF 변환 파일도 함께 첨부한다.
- 첨부파일이 5개가 넘을 경우 압축한다.

Unit 2 Email Abbreviation

이메일 약어는 시간을 절약해준다. 다음은 많이 사용하는 약어 목록이다.

한글명칭	영어 명칭
a/c	account 계좌
AM'T	amount 금액
ASAP	as soon as possible 가능한 한 빨리
Attn	Attention (우편물, 계약서의) 수신인
Ave.	Avenue 거리, 도로, -가(街) 남-북 간을 잇는 (세로)시가지 도로
Bcc	blind carbon copy 숨은 참조 동일 이메일에 있는 사람들이 서로 누가 해당 이메일을 받았는지 알리고 싶지 않을 때 사용 (예) 이메일을 50명 이상의 많은 사람들에게 보낼 때
Cc	carbon copy 참조 이메일에 대한 내용을 알려주고 싶을 때 사용. cc 수신인은 해당 이메일에 답변할 필요는 없음
Corp.	Corporation 회사
Dept.	Department 부서
Div.	Division 부서
ETD	estimated time of departure 예상출발시각
ETA	estimated time of arrival 예상도착시각
FYI	for your information 참조로(알고 계시라고)
Inc.	Incorporated 회사
MSG	Message
N/A	not applicable 해당사항 없음

한글명칭	영어 명칭
PLS	Please
RSVP	(불어) répondez s'il vous plaît = Please reply (초대장에서) 참석여부에 대한 회답을 바랍니다
Q'TY	quantity 수량
St.	Street 거리, 도로, -가(街) 동-서 간을 잇는 (가로)시가지 도로
w/	with
w/o	without
wk	week

Unit 3

Key Expressions Used in Email

〈시작 문구〉

- 9월 30일자 요청에 대하여 이메일 드립니다.

  I am emailing you regarding your request dated September 30th.

- 6월 1일자 답신 잘 받았습니다.

  Thank you for your reply dated June 1st.

- 이 이메일이 잘 전달되길 바랍니다.

  I hope this email finds you well.

- 오늘 의논했던 프로젝트 관련하여 메일 드립니다.

  I am writing in reference to the project we discussed earlier today.

- 빠른 회신 감사드립니다

  Thank you for your quick reply.

- 큰 도움에 감사드립니다.

  I am grateful for your great support.

- 다음 회의는 화요일에 개최될 예정이니 참고해 주시기 바랍니다.

  Please note that the next meeting will be held on Tuesday.

- 첨부파일을 참고해 주시기 바랍니다.

  Please see (find) the attached.

- 참고로, 아래 메일과 첨부파일을 전달해 드립니다.

  FYI, I am forwarding the below email and attachments.

- 상세내용은 다음과 같습니다.

  Details are as follows.

〈마무리 문구〉

- 요청하신 모든 자료를 포함하여 첨부파일을 보냅니다.

  I am enclosing an attachment which contains all the information you requested.

- 요청하신 파일을 첨부하였습니다.

  Please find the attached file you requested.

- 당신의 답장을 기대하겠습니다.
  I look forward to hearing from you.
- 가능한 빨리 회신 주시면 감사하겠습니다.
  I would appreciate your prompt reply.
- 우리 제안에 빠른 답변을 기대하겠습니다.
  I look forward to your prompt response to our offer.
- 궁금한 점 있으시면 언제든 주저 마시고 질문해 주세요.
  Please do not hesitate to contact me if you have any questions.
  Please ask me at any time if you have any more questions.
- 추가적인 정보가 필요하시면 언제든 연락 주세요.
  If you need any further information, Please do not hesitate to contact us.
- 언제든 자유롭게 의견 주세요.
  Please feel free to give us your feedback.
- 앞으로도 계속해서 제안해 주시기 바랍니다.
  Please keep us updated on other proposals you offer.
- 제가 11월 1일부터 3일까지 사무실을 비우게 됨을 유념해 주시기 바랍니다.
  Please note that I will be out of the office from November 1st to 3rd .
- 당신의 수고에 다시 한번 감사드립니다.
  Thanks again for your effort.
- 시간 내주셔서 감사합니다.
  Thank you for your time and consideration.
- 당신의 협조에 감사드립니다.
  Thank you for all of your cooperation.
- 불편을 드려 죄송합니다.
  Sorry for any inconvenience.

〈긍정적인 답변〉

- 그 문제가 해결되었음을 알려드립니다.
  We are pleased to inform you that we solved the issue.
- 당신의 제안을 수락함을 알려드리게 되어 기쁩니다.
  I am pleased to inform you that we have accepted your offer.

〈부정적인 답변〉

- 죄송하지만 귀하의 제안을 수락하기 어려울 것 같습니다.
  We are sorry to inform you that we are unable to accept your offer.
- 죄송하지만 미팅에 참석이 힘들겠습니다.
  I regret to say that I won't be able to attend the meeting.

- 안타깝지만 그날은 이미 다른 일정이 잡혀있어서 회의 참석이 힘듭니다.
  Unfortunately, we already have plans for that day, so we won't be able to attend the conference.

Unit 4 Sample Email Templates

① Thank-you email

[E-mail]

To:	Minsoo Yoon <minsoo_Yoon@abc.com>
From:	Yoona Kim <Kim_yoona@xyz.com>
Date:	July 2, 2022
Subject:	Last week's meeting w/ XYZ company
Attachment:	Catalog

Dear Ms. Yoon,

Thank you for taking the time to meet with me last week. It was nice to meet you.

I'm glad we had the opportunity to discuss the issue. As promised, I have enclosed our most recent catalog. If you have any questions, please do not hesitate to contact me at 010-123-4567.

I look forward to working with you.

Best regards,
Yoona Kim
Xyz Company

Enclosure

❷ Invitation email

[E-mail]

To:	Peter Ranger <P.Ranger@abc.com>
Cc:	Mary Kim<Mary_Kim@xyz.com>
From:	John Smith <JohnSmith@xyz.com>
Date:	December 6, 2021
Subject:	Invitation for XYZ Company's 5th Anniversary Party
Attachment:	Invitation card

Dear Mr. Ranger,

Please see the enclosed. If you have any questions, please do not hesitate to contact me.

Best regards,
John Smith

Enclosure

〈Enclosure: Invitation Card〉

XYZ Company's 5th Anniversary Party

XYZ Company celebrates its 5th anniversary on January 6, 2022

Please join us and enjoy the party.

Time: Thursday, January 6, 2022 at 6:30 p.m.

Place: Rose Hall, OKim's Hotel

RSVP to Mary Kim

Mary_Kim@xyz.com, 02-123-4567

③ Request email (1)

[E-mail]

To:	hyesoo Cha <hyesoo_Cha@cheil.com>
Cc:	Yunji Kim, Director <yunjikim@cheil.com>
From:	Sungmin Lim <Lim_sungmin@cheil.com>
Date:	July 2, 2022
Subject:	Attachment Error
Attachment:	Video conference schedule

Dear Hyesoo,

Thanks for e-mailing me the details of the video conference, but the attached file does not open properly. Could you please resend it?

Regards,
Sungmin Lim

❹ Request email (2)

➡ 보내기 | 미리보기 | 임시저장 | 내게쓰기

받는사람 ☐ 개인별 ? contact@aceedu.com

참조 jayking@aceedu.com

숨은참조 hypark@globalen.com

보내는 이름 susan_kim@globalen.com

제목 ☐ 중요 ! request for education program information

파일첨부 내 PC | 네이버 MYBOX

☐ 파일명

☐ 210825세미나자료.PDF

삭제

To Whom It May Concern,

Could you please tell me about your upcoming educational program, or send me a brochure?
Thank you in advance for any information you can provide.

Best Regards,
Susan Kim

____

Susan Kim

Global Enterprise

#55, SEJONG STREET, JUNG GU,
SEOUL, REPUBLIC OF KOREA 100-716
https://www.globalen.com
Tel. 82-2-360-1357 / Mobile. 010-xxxx-xxxx

Answer Key

Chapter 1 Greetings & Introductions

Practicing on Your Own

A. Complete the sentences with ***is***, ***am***, or ***are***.

1. He **is** at work.
2. They **are** at home.
3. I **am** in class.
4. She **is** on the bus.
5. They **are** from Japan.
6. It **is** on the desk.
7. You **are** from India.
8. I **am** twenty.
9. You **are** so friendly.
10. It **is** Saturday.

B. Rewrite these sentences with ***he***, ***she***, ***it*** or ***they***.

1. Mary is a student. — **She is a student**.
2. Tom is at work. — **He is at work**.
3. Peter and Tom are students. — **They are students**.

4. The windows are open. **They are open**.
5. Today is Friday. **It is Friday**.

Language Check

A. Match each question with the correct answer.

a. Where are you from? **(iii)**	i. Yes, I have.
b. What do you do? **(iv)**	ii. Yes, I do.
c. Who do you work for? **(v)**	iii. I'm from Japan.
d. Where do you live? **(vi)**	v. I'm an engineer.
e. Have you ever been to Korea? **(i)**	v. IBM.
f. Do you like Seoul? **(ii)**	vi. An-Yang city

B. Write the questions in the Simple Present Tense.

Ex. Who / work for? (you)
Who do you work for?

a. What / do? (your brother)
What does your brother do?

b. Where / work? (you)
Where do you work?

c. How old / be? (they)
How old are they?

d. What / do in your spare time? (you)
What do you do in your spare time?

e. Where / be from? (your parents)
Where are your parents from?

Chapter 2 Daily Routines at the Office

Practicing on Your Own

Look at the site map and complete the sentences using the diagrams in the above.

a. Information Center is **on the left of** the main gate.

b. Rest Room is **between** Gift Shop **and** Drug Store.

c. Snack Bar is **next to** Office Supplies.

d. Drug Store is **on the right of** the main gate.

e. ABC Company is **behind** Office Supplies.

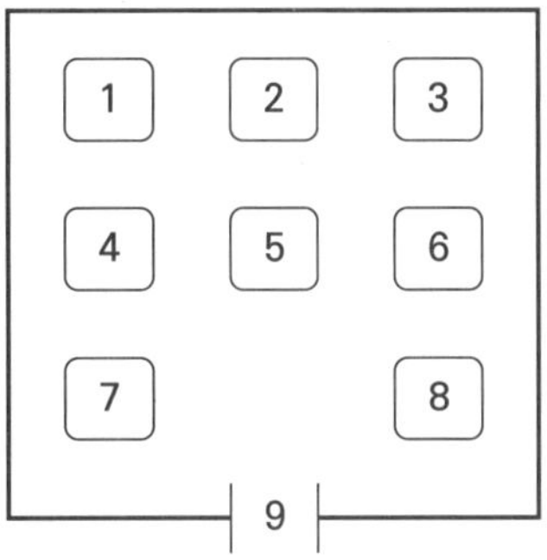

1 Snack Bar

2 Office Supplies

3 Gift Shop

4 Restaurant

5 ABC Company

6 Rest Room

7 Information center

8 Drug Store

9 Main Gate

Language Check

Match the meanings of the phrases in bold letters to the explanations on the right side.

a. to take someone into a vehicle (2)

b. The coffee shop is opposite side of our building. (3)

c. He is standing ahead of me. (4)

d. the floor of a building underground (1)

1. basement
2. pick up
3. across from
4. in front of

Chapter 3 Business Telephoning

Practicing on Your Own

A. Complete the following sentences with the correct prepositions.

1. I'll see you __**at**__ three o'clock.
2. I'll see you __**on**__ Wednesday.
3. I can make it __**in**__ the morning.
4. I can't make it __**on**__ Monday afternoon.
5. I can't make it __**on**__ on September 2nd.
6. We can meet __**in**__ May.
7. I can't make it __**at**__ 3:30.
8. Can you make it __**in**__ the evening.
9. No, but I'm free __**in**__ the morning

B. Write the questions out correctly.

Ex. : (calling / who / is?)

__**Who's calling? It's John**__ .

1. (speak / who / did / to / you?) I spoke to the department manager.
   __**Who did you speak to**__ ?
2. (this evening / coming / who / is?) Just our two Japanese agents.
   __**Who is coming this evening**__ ?
3. (left / who / briefcase / a / here / yesterday?) I did.
   __**Who left a briefcase here yesterday**__ ?
4. (is / boss / your / who?) Kathrin Mathys.
   __**Who is your boss**__ ?
5. (you / report / do / who / to?) I report to Kathrin Mathys.
   __**Who do you report to**__ ?

C. In the following conversation , choose the most suitable response.

A Hello, is that accounts?
B **Yes, it is.** / I am.

A I'd like to speak to Sara Adams, please.
B I am / **This is** Sara Adams.

A Hello, my name is Jessica Brown from ABC Company.
I call / **I'm calling** about a bill we sent you.
B Oh, you should speak to my colleague, Roger Simons. I'll put you through to his extension.

A Thank you.
B The line's busy. Are you holding? / **Will you hold?**

A Yes, I am / **I will.**
B I'm afraid the line is still busy. Would / **Could** you give me your number and I / **I'll** ask him to call you again / **back?**

A Yes, certainly. It's 568-9839.
B Thank you. Goodbye.

A Goodbye.

Language Check

A. Match the verbs with the objects.

a. to dial (iii)	i. a phone
b. to make (iv)	ii. a message
c. to leave (ii)	iii. a number
d. to use (i)	iv. a call

B. Match the meanings of the phrases in bold letters to the explanations on the right side.

a. **Who's calling** please? (v)	i. busy
b. I'll just **put you through.** (iv)	ii. wait (on the phone)

c. Would you like to **hold**? (ii)

d. I can't **make** the meeting next Monday. (iii)

e. I'm **tied up** all day. (i)

iii. come to

iv. make the connection for you

v. What's your name?

Chapter 4 Meeting Arrangement

Practicing on Your Own

A. Refer to the chart in the above and complete each sentence with ***in***, ***on***, or ***at***.

1. His office is __**on**__ the seventh floor.
2. Susan is __**at**__ work now.
3. The office building is __**on**__ Broad Street.
4. Peter isn't __**in**__ his office now. He's __**at**__ the bank.
5. After work, I sit __**on**__ the deck and relax.
6. Some employees of our company work __**at**__ home.
7. There are branch offices __**in**__ Taiwan and Japan.
8. He works __**in**__ Seoul.

B. Complete the following sentences using the prepositions of time, ***for*** or ***until***.

1. I'll be away __**for**__ five days.
2. I'll be away __**until**__ the end of this month.
3. You must finish the report __**untll**__ this weekend.
4. I'm going on a business trip __**for**__ two weeks.

Language Check

Here is Gina Kim's diary for the week.

Monday	Tuesday	Wednesday	Thursday	Friday
12.30: lunch with Joe	10.00 sales meeting	10.00 factory visit	8.00 flight to Paris	

Complete Gina Kim's description of her appointments with the correct prepositions from the list. In three of spaces no preposition is necessary.

on	in	at	to	with	for

1. **X** Today I'm having lunch **with** Joe.
2. **X** Tomorrow morning **at** ten I'm going **to** a sales meeting.
3. I'm visiting **X** the factory **on** Wednesday **in** the morning.
4. I'm flying **to** Paris **for** the training course **on** Friday **at** 8 a.m.

Chapter 5 Business Trip

Practicing on Your Own

A. Complete the sentences. Choose the correct numbers.

1. My classroom is on the **second** (two, second) floor.
2. My **first** (one, first) class is at nine-thirty.
3. Sue is **twenty-three** (twenty-three, twenty-third) years old.
4. The bookstore is on **Fifth** (Five, Fifth) Avenue.
5. **Three** Three (Three, Third) apples are green, and **six** (six, sixth) are red.
6. November is the **eleventh** (eleven, eleventh) month of the year.

B. Complete the sentences. Use the correct form of the verbs and the adverbs of frequency in parentheses.

1. Lulu __**is often**__ (be, often) early. She __**usually waits**__ (wait, usually) for other people.
2. Pete __**is often**__ (be, often) late He __**rarely gets**__ (get, rarely) to work on time.
3. Elenore __**is usually**__ (be, usually) on time. She __**rarely comes**__ (come, rarely) late.
4. Norma __**is always**__ (be, always) early for meetings.
5. Carol is like her father. She __**is usually**__ (be, usually) late for everything.

Language Check

A. Match the questions on the left with the best response on the right.

c	1. What do you do?	a. No, I'm from China.
f	2. Do you like it here?	b. For one month.
a	3. Are you from Japan?	c. I'm an engineer.
b	4. How long have you been here?	d. Yes, I have two kids.
d	5. Do you have any children?	e. I'm afraid it's too hot and humid for me.
e	6. How do you like this weather?	f. Yes, I like here very much.

B. Complete each question to fit the answer provided.

Ex. Q: What is your name?

A: My name is John Smith.

1. Q: What **do you do** ?

   A: I'm an engineer. I work for Ace Computer.

2. Q: How **old are your children** ?

   A: My daughter is 15 and my boy is 11.

3. Q: How **do you like the weather** ?

   A: Very much! I love the weather here.

4. Q: How long **have you been here** ?

   A: I've been here for about six months.

저자 약력

김숙경
- 서울여자대학교 영문학 학사
- 미국 캘리포니아주립대학(UC Santa Cruz) TESOL석사
- (현) ACE 커리어 컨설팅 대표
- 대림대학교 비서행정학과 겸임교수
- ㈜ 서빈 SVC 교육실장
- 미국 캘리포니아 쿠퍼티노 교육청 이중언어 자문위원
- 미국 캘리포니아 써니베일 ESL School 강사

양혜련
- 이화여자대학교 비서학 학사
- 이화여자대학교 비서학 석사
- 서울대학교 농산업교육과 박사수료
- (현) 수원여자대학교 비서과 / 오피스매니저과 교수
- ㈜삼안인터내셔널 머천다이저
- 한국무역협회 무역실무과정 수료
- 이화여자대학교 국제회의전문가과정 연구원

Daily Office English Conversation
사무영어회화

초판 1쇄 인쇄 2022년 3월 2일
초판 1쇄 발행 2022년 3월 5일

저 자	김숙경·양혜련
펴낸이	임 순 재
펴낸곳	(주)한올출판사
등 록	제11-403호
주 소	서울시 마포구 모래내로 83(성산동 한올빌딩 3층)
전 화	(02) 376-4298(대표)
팩 스	(02) 302-8073
홈페이지	www.hanol.co.kr
e-메일	hanol@hanol.co.kr
ISBN	979-11-6647-200-8

Daily Office English Conversation
사무영어회화